THOG'S GUIDE

50,000 YEARS OF ACCOUNTING BASICS FOR THE FUTURE

"After being an accounting educator for over thirty years, I now have a whole new perspective from *Thog's Guide*. It is a must read for any serious accounting student, faculty, practitioner, or regulator."

—Michael Diamond, Vice President and Executive Vice Provost, University of Southern California

"An engaging and entertaining book – a philosophical and historical exploration of why accounting is central to any society based on commerce. *Thog's Guide* offers a glimpse of current work aimed to reformulate economics on the basis of ideas from physics and biology – and all through the eyes of a charming family of hunter-gatherer-accountants. I never had so much unexpected fun nor learned so much from a book about a subject I didn't even know I was interested in."

—Lee Smolin, Perimeter Institute for Theoretical Physics

"Physics has Brownian motion and now economics has Brownian accounting, as a family of hunter-gatherers teaches a team of real complexity scientists the importance of back to basics accounting in economic modeling. *Thog's Guide* is a light-hearted read, but it promises a serious breakthrough – the ability to test the consequences of our financial and accounting regulations in virtual reality before trying them out on you and me."

—Alfred R. Berkeley, Former President and Vice-Chairman of NASDAQ, Chairman and CEO, Pipeline Trading

First Writing, 5000 BC
First Printing, AD 1456
This Edition, AD 2005

ISBN 0-9764694-0-5
Printed in the United States of America
Published by Thogian Press
Order through MAC Productions
PO Box 84, Duvall, WA 98019
1-866-844-8406
MAC.productions@gte.net
1-425-844-9245 (fax)

THOG'S GUIDE TO QUANTUM ECONOMICS

50,000 YEARS OF ACCOUNTING BASICS FOR THE FUTURE

by Mike Brown and Zoe-Vonna Palmrose
Illustrations by Warren Miller

Acknowledgments

Thog's Guide owes its conceptual existence to Stuart Kauffman, Ray Kurzweil, Jim Herriot, Bruce Sawhill, Sasha Outkin, and Jim Anderson. Serious and outstanding scientists, not only were they extraordinarily patient with the scientific bumblings of two accountants trying to bridge the gap between the discipline of science and the art of accounting, they were good enough sports to permit us to use their real names in this fictional work. (While this is a work of fiction, it does include a few facts thanks to the assistance of our researchers, Nate Wood and Jingjing Yao.)

Thog's Guide owes its physical existence to our agent, Loretta Barrett, who believed in Thog from the beginning, our editor, Phyllis Hatfield, who breathed life into the story, and our creative director and production designer, Barbara Witt, who figured out how to capture and package the essence of the book.

The story was shaped in no small measure by our reviewers. They are accountants Mike Diamond, Mike Duffy, Bill Kinney, Roger Martin, Mark Nelson, and Dave Pearson; scientists Henry Bone, Bob Burk, and Lee Smolin; and businesspersons Al Berkeley, Bonnie Binkert, Tom Corddry,

Alexandra Featherstone, Wally Gudgell, Alan Honick, Ed Iacobucci, Mary Ladner, Jerry Masters, Barbara McKeon, and Ralph Saul.

We owe a special debt of gratitude to Warren Miller, who convinced us to keep going when it looked like *Thog's Guide* might never be printed, and drew cartoons to urge us along. And we thank our spouses, Lee and John, who were patient supporters of the Thogs throughout.

Finally, we are indebted to the Thogs themselves, who reminded us that the past holds much accounting wisdom for the future. Plus they taught us that it's OK to have a little fun when trying to figure stuff out, even if you are an accountant.

Despite all this help, we remain solely responsible for any scientific and historical misstatements and omissions in the story, as well as the outlandish accounting suggestions that it contains.

Mike Brown
Zoe-Vonna Palmrose
San Juan Islands, 2004

Contents

CONTENTS

Foreword

The recent discovery in New Mexico of a family of 50,000-year-old hunter-gatherer bookkeepers has created consternation in accounting, economic, and science circles. The Thogs, a family of four – father, mother, and two children – are reported to be living somewhere in the mountains outside Santa Fe. To protect the public from dangerous Thogian views, the Securities Exchange Commission is keeping their exact location secret while they conduct a full investigation.

The Thogs were discovered by a renegade group of accountants and complexity scientists who claim that the Thogs invented bookkeeping in the first place. They also claim that bookkeeping is the physics of complexity science economics – what they call quantum economics – and that accounting, like physics, is inherently uncertain.

Anthropologists are furiously debating how it is possible for the Thogs to have been alive this long, despite the family's testimony that they remember hunting saber-tooth tiger and mastodon.

Traditional economic historians have dismissed them entirely: "The Thogs are a silly hoax," said one, "simply too implausible to dignify with serious academic comment."

The Federal Reserve Board has positioned itself above the fray. In recent testimony to Congress, its chairman dismissed the role of bookkeepers: "After all, they only add and subtract debits and credits, which are quite simple. Rest assured, it takes a trained economist to explain the actual economy."

The Securities and Exchange Commission, however, is taking the situation seriously. Its enforcement division has subpoenaed the Thogs, seeking a cease-and-desist order, fines, and other remedies. Its chairman explained, "Accountants breaking the rules are always invoking some uncertainty mumbo jumbo to divert attention from their conflicts of interest. There is nothing uncertain about the accounting rules. They are the basis of reliable financial statements, and we will continue to aggressively prosecute those who undermine them."

Flying saucer aficionados in nearby Roswell have also joined the debate. They claim the Thogs are extraterrestrial beings who arrived in a space capsule, proof once again of a decades-long U.S. Air Force cover-up.

Meanwhile your authors, Mike Brown, former chairman of NASDAQ and past CFO of Microsoft, and Zoe-Vonna Palmrose, USC Professor of Accounting, figure prominently amongst the renegade group of accountants and complexity scientists who discovered the Thogs. Along with a biologist, a particle physicist, a computer scientist, and an economist, they interviewed the Thogs, and on the pages that follow you will read their story – the story of bookkeeping's role in complexity science and a new kind of economics – quantum economics.

I'm Warren Miller. I've taken Mike and Zoe-Vonna's records of the Thog family interviews and printed out some of the pictures for you, having made a few touch-ups with my own supply of India ink.

Before you begin reading the story, let me offer a word on terminology. As you know, physicists, biologists, computer scientists, economists, and accountants all speak different languages. The Thogs are no exception, although their terms are so simple they even make sense to an old ski bum like me. To help you with the jargon, Thogian terms are displayed in the text in *italics* the first time the Thogs explain them for you, and you'll find their definitions and accounting, economic, and scientific synonyms in the *Thogesaurus* at the back of the book.

I shouldn't hint at the plot, but I can tell you that I made it through the whole book by keeping my weight on my outside ski and using a little common sense in the steep parts. Skiing like this was all it took to Zipf through the deepest power laws without getting too dizzy from the quantum stuff.

Warren Miller
San Juan Islands, WA 2004

Dramatis Personae

Warren Miller: Filmmaker, cartoonist, and ski bum turned complexity scientist.

Thog: 50,000-year-old hunter-gatherer.

Mrs. Thog: Inventor of bookkeeping and debits and credits, discoverer of zero.

Thogette: Inventor of writing, arithmetic, banks, stock markets.

Junior: Inventor of assembly lines, statistics.

Fibonacci: (alias Leonardo) Mathematician, the father of combinatorial statistics, author of the first known book on double-entry accounting.

Mike Brown (Brownie): Former chairman of the NASDAQ stock market, with a checkered past: once CFO of Microsoft, an accounting standard-setter of sorts, a partner in the accounting firm Deloitte and Touche, a commercial fisherman.

Zoe-Vonna Palmrose (Dr. Z): Professor of Accounting, University of Southern California.

Stuart Kauffman (Stu): Biologist, MacArthur fellow, a father of the complexity science revolution.

Jim Herriot (Jim): Computer scientist.

Bruce Sawhill (Bruce): Particle physicist.

Sasha Outkin (Sasha): Economist.

Ray Kurzweil (Ray): Technologist, futurist, inventor, National Medal of Technology winner.

Chief Lion Ring: First standard-setter.

Chief Bear Ford: Second standard-setter.

Chief Left-It: Third standard-setter.

Jim Anderson: Professor of Fisheries, University of Washington.

Chapter 1

The Santa Fe Trail

In 1999 the Thogs packed their worldly belongings, closed up their cave in the Poconos, and headed down the trail for New Mexico and the mountains outside Santa Fe. Moving was nothing new for them; during the last 50,000 years they'd moved a lot.

The present move had the usual provocation: they were disturbed by trends in accounting rules. Not all hunter-gatherers move over a few accounting changes, but the Thogs are bookkeepers and like to keep an eye on accounting developments. Recessions often follow bad accounting, and experience has taught them to wait these out someplace where they can get by hunting and gathering without losing sight of the future.

Mrs. Thog would miss her tastefully decorated cave in the Poconos not far from Wall Street, but she generally looks on the bright side and was in a cheerful mood as they hiked up into the mountains.

"The vista here reminds me of the view of the Fertile Crescent from our cave in the Zagros Mountains," she said. "You remember, back in 7000 BC when we were sorting out the recordkeeping mess caused by all those clumsy clay tokens?"

"The view is similar," Thog said.

"It was a good thing Thogette invented writing and arithmetic when she did," Mrs. Thog continued. "Recordkeeping is so much easier now without the tokens."

"I certainly hope my inventions are up to the task of simplifying the current mess," Thogette said.

Thog, who unlike Mrs. Thog wasn't in a particularly good mood, harrumphed, "Arithmetic is quite up to the task."

"Particularly now that these new computers are so good at it," Mrs. Thog said.

"What's missing is the common sense to use it," he grumbled.

"Common sense does seem to fall from fashion from time to time," she replied, still agreeable.

"I believe they still consider it useful down there," Junior piped up, pointing to Santa Fe.

"The scientists perhaps," Thogette said. "I'm not so sure about the venture capitalists."

Conversing more or less in this vein, the Thogs eventually selected a cave, moved in, and made themselves comfortable by settling down to a tasty rabbit dinner.

Thog was still in a grumpy mood, which was not lost on Junior and Thogette. In a more convivial setting they might have taken the opportunity to bicker, but tonight they waited to see how their mom would handle Thog.

He wasn't grouchy because he expected trouble with the stock market. (Thogette was a little upset by the prospect, because she invented the first stock market in 1600, and was concerned about what might happen to her invention. But Thog had reassured her that her basic idea was still sound.)

He wasn't grouchy because a number of important companies in the economy were beginning to have trouble. (Junior was a little upset by this, because he invented the first assembly line in 1700, and was disappointed that his original idea wasn't working out better. But his father had reassured him as well.)

In fact, even though it caused them to move their household, Thog wasn't that upset about the current accounting situation, either. (Mrs. Thog was a little upset, because she's the one who originally invented the equal debits and credits of bookkeeping and discovered zero while trying to balance her books. But when she complained about the new accounting rules, Thog had also reassured her.)

He had pointed out that bad accounting is really nothing new. Basic bookkeeping has survived countless silly trends in the past, most of which were not unlike the current one. And besides, he'd added, these accounting rule-makers come and go.

The truth is, rabbits were making Thog grouchy.

Not how they were cooked, because Mrs. Thog is a skillful cook and rabbits are one of her specialties; her rabbit recipes are widely known in hunter-gatherer circles. Nor was it anything Thog holds against rabbits themselves. In fact in 1202, one of his good friends, a Renaissance bookkeeper named Fibonacci, did some very interesting computational work involving rabbits. Thog had discussed these computations with Fibonacci into the wee hours, and the fact that rabbits were involved never bothered him one whit.

What Thog hated is hunting rabbits, because real hunters hunt big animals like mastodon. Mastodon disappeared in 9000 BC, when the Mesolithic Age wrecked their habitat, and Thog has never quite gotten over it. He was mollified by hunting tigers for a while, but eventually tigers, too, became endangered. And now, thanks to bad accounting, he was reduced to hunting what was left – rabbits – a low blow for a proud hunter-gatherer.

Having been happily married for 49,981 years, Mrs. Thog understands her husband pretty well, so she wasn't too surprised by Thog's mood. She knew what he needed – either a distraction from rabbits, or a new challenge of some sort. Meanwhile she decided to get him out of her hair while she considered the problem.

As Thog chewed away moodily, she said, "Umm, dear, did you have any trouble hunting these lovely rabbits?"

"Of course not!" he harrumphed. "But you can hardly call it hunting. Now that mastodon are extinct, real hunting is pretty much a thing of the past."

"I was just reading about a statue of a mammoth at a place called Mammoth Mountain. A mammoth is very much like a mastodon, is it not?"

"Sure, but how challenging is it to hunt a statue? It's silly enough hunting rabbits. And this is the second time this century. We just went through this bad-accounting-rabbit-hunting cycle in 1928."

"Oh," Mrs. Thog said sweetly, "I was just thinking that perhaps you might like to travel to Mammoth Mountain and take a look at the statue, sort of for old time's sake. You never know, you might find some interesting tracks. I believe mammoths were discovered there quite recently – relatively recently, anyhow."

Thog brightened at this. "That's actually a good idea,

my dear. There's no sense moping around here waiting for the return of commonsense accounting. It usually takes a while. I'll put up a few rabbits for you and the children and then go take a look at this statue."

When Thog headed for Mammoth Mountain the next day, his family breathed a collective sigh of relief. In fact, Junior and Thogette complimented Mrs. Thog on her artful handling of their grumpy father. And it's not often that teenage children compliment their mom.

Chapter 2

The Call

My name is Mike Brown. I used to be chairman of the NASDAQ stock market. Before that I was CFO of Microsoft. Long before that I was a commercial fisherman. Now I am just retired, telling the occasional tall tale, not that unusual for a retired guy – especially a fisherman.

Back when the Thogs decided to move to Santa Fe, things still looked pretty good on Wall Street: the market was at an all time high, and the view on the street was that it had nowhere to go but up. I was in my office at NASDAQ enjoying all of this. Fortunately, I wasn't at the NYSE, where it's hard to concentrate on anything over the din on the old-fashioned trading floor. But NASDAQ is an automated market, which is much quieter, so you can actually work or talk the phone. I was working when I got the phone call that started this crazy story – a search for the truth of accounting, mad scientists, a secret laboratory, an invention called an economic particle collider, a brush with a combinatoric catastrophe, interviews with the Thog family, Warren Miller cartoons – the whole thing.

The call came from an accountant. I got a few calls from accountants back then, probably because I used to be an accountant myself and sometimes an accountant is the only one who can tell what another accountant is talking about. In fact, sometimes even another accountant can't tell. Mostly they called to complain about the accounting rules, and there are a lot of them, so if you're in the mood to complain it's not hard to work up a good list.

The caller was an accounting professor, and she began with a few of the usual complaints. But the real bee in her bonnet was something she called "the truth" of accounting and how nobody seemed to care about it but her. Hers was the first complaint I ever received on this topic. In fact, rather than try to explain, I'll just reproduce the call for you and you can see for yourself.

You may wonder how I can do this. Well, my friend Ray Kurzweil invented this very cool machine called a Kurzweil converter,* that produces both a written transcript and pictures of what it hears. He gave me a prototype to try out at NASDAQ, where he knew we had a lot of transcript work. The Kurzweil converter calls Zoe-Vonna "Dr. Z" for short, so I do too, and it calls me "Brownie," which is what Dr. Z calls me now.

Dr. Z: Hi. This is Zoe-Vonna Palmrose. I used to work with you in public accounting. I'm here in New York for a few days. You remember me, don't you?

Brownie: Yes. Hey, you don't mind if I convert this, do you? I'm trying out a cool machine that automatically converts voices to text and art.

---

* Actually, maybe he hasn't, but he might.

Dr. Z: Uhh, I guess not. Is it like recording the call?

Brownie: No, you can't listen to it again. You can only read it or see a picture of it. This is just a technology test.

Dr. Z: I see. Well, OK.

Brownie: So how are you? What are you doing these days?

Dr. Z: I'm fine. I'm a professor trying to teach accounting, but accounting is all screwed up. So actually, to be perfectly honest, I'm not fine. (voice rises) I'm not fine at all. In fact, that's why I'm calling you.

Brownie: I'm sorry to hear that. What's the problem with accounting?

Dr. Z: Well, to begin with, the rules are too complex, many of them conflict with one another, and FASB* is throwing every tradition out the window. Nobody knows what net income means anymore. The analysts are ignoring the accountants, coming up with their own measures, and who knows what else? This is hyping up the market, which will probably crash. Are you taking my point?

Brownie: Yes, I believe I am. But I'm not sure there is much we can do to help you here at NASDAQ, although, of course, we would prefer that the market not crash.

Dr. Z: Yes, yes. I know. Actually, that's not my point. There's the audit profession, which is going down the tubes. Have you thought about that? You do like having your issuers audited, don't you?

---

* FASB ("faz-bee") is accounting-speak for the Financial Accounting Standards Board, which makes the accounting rules on behalf of the SEC. FASB rules apply to both public and non-public companies that are audited.

Brownie: Of course we do. But I'm not sure how you think we can help. Our listing rules already require audits.

Dr. Z: I'm not calling because I expect NASDAQ to do anything. I'm calling because you were supposed to be an accountant once and aren't anymore, so I thought maybe you could think about accounting without thinking like an accountant.

Brownie: I see. Well, I wasn't very good at accounting. I had to find other work.

Dr. Z: Good for you. (takes a deep breath) Worst of all, there are fewer and fewer students signing up for accounting classes. We're not getting the best and the brightest. Do you know how accounting is viewed in a university? Well, let me tell you – at the bottom of the barrel. If you tell someone you're a scientist, they think you're smart. But if you tell them you're an accountant, they not only think you're dumb, they think you're boring and probably dishonest to boot. If the smart kids won't go into accounting, then accounting will go down the tubes just like auditing. Mark my words!

Brownie: That doesn't sound too good. But your point isn't completely clear. How do you expect me to help?

Dr. Z: Yes, let me get to the point. The point is debits and credits!

Brownie: (incredulous) What? That's your point?

Dr. Z: (assertive) Yes – you heard me. Debits and credits. What exactly are they?

Brownie: Debits and credits? They're the things you keep by the window and the door – like in the old joke.

Dr. Z: Come on. Haven't you ever wondered about their true significance?

Brownie: Sometimes it's easier not to.

Dr. Z: May I quote you on that in my monograph—"NASDAQ Chairman tells old jokes while accounting flounders?"

Brownie: I would prefer that you didn't, of course.

Dr. Z: OK, then. So what are we going to do about it?

Brownie: We? What are we going to do about debits and credits?

Dr. Z: That's right – we.

Brownie: Have you talked to other accountants about this?

Dr. Z: No. They're all preoccupied with rules. They don't care about searching for the fundamental truth of accounting.

Brownie: I see. Well, you might try a scientist; they say they search for fundamental truths.

Dr. Z: OK, so do you know one?

Brownie: Well, I know a biologist in Santa Fe – a complexity scientist, actually – who helped us develop a computer model to predict the consequences of proposed NASDAQ trading rules. I'll call and see if he knows any scientists you can talk to.

Dr. Z: Fine, but I'm not going to go meet them all by myself. You'll have to go along and introduce me.

Brownie: And if I agree to do that, you won't quote me in your monograph?

Chapter 3

Dr. Z's Diary

As promised, I called my friend Stu Kauffman in Santa Fe. I described my Dr. Z problem to him. He was sympathetic. A sophisticated scientist, he is sensitive to the ramifications of bad press. I told him I needed to bring her to Santa Fe to interview some scientists about debits and credits. Almost any scientists would do.

"Debits and credits, like in bookkeeping?" Stu asked.

"Yes."

"I'm thinking," he said, after a while.

Stu told me he planned to go hiking in the mountains for a week. Could it wait until after that? He wanted to think about it some more. (Stu likes thinking.) I explained that I needed to get this over with soon. Didn't he know any scientists who could help me out right away?

"I'm not sure," he said. "I can't really think of science and bookkeeping together somehow."

I understood the problem, I said, but I didn't think Dr. Z would be very picky.

More silence. He was still thinking.

"I can't really think of science and bookkeeping together somehow."

Finally, he said he was working with an interdisciplinary team at some place called the Particle Economics Research Institute – PartEcon. The team included a particle physicist and a computer scientist plus an economist who was actually a physicist and had become interested in economics. Apparently some of his former colleagues considered economic work to be unbecoming scientific conduct.

I suggested that accountants are familiar with unbecoming conduct and said I didn't think Dr. Z would be put off by it.

"Oh, the unbecoming conduct is just a sidebar," he said, "the gist of their work is quantum economics."

"Quantum economics?"

"Ah yes, reminds me of the good old days in Copenhagen," he said.

Wherever, I thought. (Stu sometimes goes unexpected places in a conversation, if you know what I mean.)

Stu explained that if scientists understood the atomic structure of economics – quantum economics – they might be able to explain the emergence of producers and consumers, and how their interactions result in the emergence of money. Eventually, scientists might even be able to explain why the economy is dynamic, with volatile cycles, and not in equilibrium, a static state, which economists like to assume in their models even though it doesn't appear to exist.

Stu lost me, mostly, but I guessed that this quantum stuff could help economists explain what's going on better, and this would be a big improvement, since from my perch at NASDAQ, it looked to me like most of the time economists didn't have a clue.

"Quantum economics is the search for economic truth," Stu continued, warming to the topic. "Of course, one can't tell in advance where such a search will lead. Do you think Dalton was looking for a spare part in a nuclear power plant – a spring or something – when he formalized atomic theory? Of course not!"

"Hey, Stu, speaking of truth," I interrupted, "do you think maybe quantum economics might be connected to the truth of debits and credits?"

This stumped him. He wasn't sure. Not that it couldn't be, of course. It would be paradoxical – bookkeeping and the quantum together – but quantum stuff is very paradoxical.

"I suppose it's possible," he finally concluded. "Not likely, but possible."

Well, they sounded connected to me – money, debits, credits, and economic truth – and after a life on Wall Street, I wasn't about to be sidetracked by a little paradox. I decided to roll with it. Everyone knows a thing that sounds right will often satisfy a troublesome accountant.

"Can you set up a meeting with these quantum guys later this week?"

"I'll see what I can do."

The next day Stu called back. He had arranged for us to meet the two scientists and their economist friend, but they were very secretive about their work and we could not disclose what they told us. I promised we wouldn't.

A few days later, I met Dr. Z at the airport ticket counter. She was struggling to check an immense backpack. All I had was a small carry-on with the Kurzweil converter. The pack was full of reference books, she explained – background for our meeting.

There went my plan for a quick and simple trip with carry-ons only.

On the plane, Dr. Z prepared for our upcoming meeting by reading *At Home in the Universe* by Stuart Kauffman. She said she wanted to learn more about him. I explained he wasn't going to be there, but she kept reading.

I prepared by taking a nap. Bill Gates taught me that taking a nap is a good way to get organized. (I don't put the blanket over my head like he does, though.)

When the flight attendant woke me up for landing, I noticed Dr. Z was making notes in a little book that had an equation on its cover: "*Debits + Credits = Zero*."

"What have you got there?" I asked.

"Oh, it's my diary," she replied. "I've been keeping a record of my quest for the true meaning of debits and credits."

"No kidding? How long have you been doing this?"

"Since 1966."

"May I see?"

"Well, actually it's private."

"C'mon. Debits and credits? How private can they be?"

"You might be surprised." (As it turned out, I was.)

"How about just the first entry in 1966, then?" I said. "I mean, after all, you asked me to help. Shouldn't I have some idea of how you got started on all this in the first place?"

"Well ... all right," she said. "But you have to respect my privacy. I'm serious."

"Of course."

Here's Dr. Z's first diary entry. (It may not seem like we're respecting her privacy, but you should see what we left out.)

Dear Diary,

I'm glad no one but me will ever read this. They wouldn't understand. I fell in love today. I'm just sure it's the real thing!

I fell in love with the accounting equation. My accounting professor (who is very cute!!) just walked in and wrote it on the board. It's sooo elegant!!! It's like it captures, well, I don't know, something very important.

The class was trying to understand all this and it was getting really exciting, when the professor suddenly said, "OK, we have some rules to learn, so if you're still a little confused, just remember 'debits by the window and credits by the door.'" Everyone laughed. Then we moved on – just like that!

Well, I don't think this is a laughing matter. I just know there is something deeper here!!! Maybe if I major in accounting I can figure it out? I'm going to talk to my advisor first thing tomorrow.

"Wow," I said, beginning the next entry. "It gets better. Look at this one. Would you believe …"

"Give me that!" she said, snatching it back.

Chapter 4

The Secret Laboratory

In Santa Fe we picked up a rental car. I drove while Dr. Z navigated the complicated and circuitous route to the secret laboratory – PartEcon – the home of quantum economics. Here we would meet the scientists, Jim Herriot, a computer guru, Bruce Sawhill, a particle physicist, and the economist, Sasha Outkin.

After about an hour, Dr. Z decided we were lost. She suggested we stop and ask directions. Like most guys, I didn't. Besides, it wouldn't be a secret laboratory if everyone knew where it was. We were arguing about this when Dr. Z reached over and turned on the Kurzweil converter:

Brownie: Hey, what are you doing?

Dr. Z: I think the converter likes being on. How would you like it if someone could just turn you off whenever they felt like it?

Brownie: (stops the car) Hey look. Here it is! See, we weren't lost after all.

Dr. Z: Oh no! There has to be some mistake. This can't be it. Just look at it. It's dilapidated. The paint's peeling off. The windows are boarded up. There's no way this can be an economics laboratory. No way!

Brownie: Well, it does look secret, and we've come this far. Let's at least check it out.

"Jim, you really ought to wear your safety gear in case we have a combinatoric catastrophe."

I carried the converter, Dr. Z struggled with her backpack and we approached the building. We knocked several times but got no answer. We heard loud music coming from the laboratory and I assumed they couldn't hear us over the music.

When I turned the knob, the door opened and we peeked in. Just as Stu promised, there were three guys, all absorbed in what they were doing. Since they didn't notice us at first, we had a chance to look the situation over.

In the center of the laboratory stood a contraption that emitted a low hum, audible despite the music. It was – well, I'll come back to the contraption. Let me start with the people.

The first guy was barefoot and sitting hunched over a console that was connected to the contraption by a tangle of wires. The console sat on a table crowded with computer screens and keyboards, along with a toaster, a pair of shoes, a tub of butter, and two cases of English muffins. He was typing furiously, munching muffins and talking to himself, while the toaster periodically popped up another muffin.

Another guy was tinkering with what looked like a monitoring device that was connected to the contraption. He wore what appeared to be a biohazard suit complete with a safety visor, and in contrast to his barefoot colleague, he wore safety shoes.

The third guy stood at a whiteboard that was covered with graphs and equations – a mind-boggling array of characters and symbols, all written small in a crimped hand. He was frenetically drawing more graphs.

The music came from an electronic organ in the corner

playing Bach. (I learned later it was Bach, but I could tell right away it wasn't the Rolling Stones.) There was no organist at the keyboard.

Dr. Z guessed the guy at the console must be the computer scientist, Jim Herriot. She thought the one drawing graphs was probably the economist, Sasha Outkin, since economists like graphs. This meant the one in the hazard suit must be Bruce Sawhill, the particle physicist. We were too far away to hear what they were saying. But the converter was able to pick up their conversation:

Jim: Hmm … Why is this thing still so deep in the ordered regime? I guess we need to get more of these economic functions in here. I sure hope this function generator will do the trick.

(I later learned that in complexity science, a space of possibilities for interactions of fundamental particles has three parts: one is called the ordered regime (which is sort of a frozen place); another is the chaotic regime (which is what it sounds like); and the third – the space between them – is called the edge of chaos.)

Bruce: I'll tell you Jim, we gotta be careful. I mean, this baby could go combinatoric in a blink. If we're not careful, we're gonna have a full catastrophe on our hands – complete chaos – and you'll wish we were back in the ordered regime. Oh yes you will.

(Bruce later explained that a nuclear blast is very much like a combinatoric explosion.)

Jim: Relax. Have some toast.

Bruce: If you'd worked where I used to work, you wouldn't be so cavalier. No you wouldn't.

"Some guys will do anything to be in a Warren Miller ski movie."

(Bruce used to work at Los Alamos where they made bombs and is still a little jumpy about things like critical mass and powerful combinatorics.)

Sasha: Bruce is right. Oh my! Whatever will we do if these economic functions push things over the edge of chaos?

Jim: Relax, Sasha. So far this thing has stayed frozen solid – locked up. Bruce, why don't you take over on the keyboard and play something quiet and soothing for Sasha while I tune up this new function generator?

(Bruce does play the organ. He's a serious pipe organist and gives concerts some Sundays. He says music restores his psychic balance after making bombs.)

Bruce: The organ's playing Bach's Toccata and Fugue in D Minor, which is soothing. And the volume's an important security precaution – it blankets the collider hum. But if you insist, I'll turn it down a little.

Jim: All right, I think I've got the function generator working now. Let's try this thing again.

Bruce: OK, but don't go pushing that collide button until I get the emergency shutdown gear in place.

This is when the scientists noticed us and we introduced ourselves. Dr. Z had guessed their specialties correctly. And yes, they were expecting us and would be happy to discuss their work. In fact, Jim said they were at a good place to take a break and talk right then.

Chapter 5

Quantum Economics

We pulled up chairs around the contraption. It continued to hum ominously, and Bruce explained they were worried about a combinatoric catastrophe, so I kept a respectful distance from it. Jim offered us toast. I asked what they were working on. Jim confirmed Stu's report that whatever it is, it's called quantum economics.

"Quantum economics will have practical benefits," Sasha said. "Someday it will help explain important economic events that economists observe but don't understand – like Schumpeterian gales."

I thought these might be some sort of Santa Fe meteorological phenomena,* but before I could ask about them, Dr. Z asked what "quantum" means.

"Hmm," Bruce said thoughtfully. "It's derived from quanta, which are very small chunks of energy that interact in what's called a quantum state. But how to sum up a quantum state? Well, in such a state each possible property of a fundamental particle is ambiguous, which is a yes <u>and</u> no condition. Take a particle's location, for example. In a quan-

---

*It turns out they are economic weather events like the Great Depression, the Dot Com Bomb, etc.

tum state the particle is in one specific location and in all other possible locations at the same time. Its properties remain ambiguous like this until the asking of a question via an experiment causes the particle to 'decide' what yes or no properties it has. This process is called disambiguation, or quantum decoherence. Most people find all this very confusing. But this quantum description of the world of physical measurement has been extensively confirmed in numerous scientific experiments."

"I see," said Dr. Z, who probably didn't, but I didn't either, so I let is slide.

"Tell me about your experiment," I suggested, pointing to the contraption and hoping to move on past disambiguation.

I'll let the Kurzweil converter take it from here:

Bruce: (beams proudly) This baby is an economic particle collider.

Dr. Z: What do you do with it?

Bruce: We invented it to conduct experiments to discover the atomic structure of economics.

Dr. Z: How will you know when you find it?

Sasha: That will be when our computer model – the collider – produces results that look like the real economy. First we should see a primitive economy emerging: producers and consumers resulting from particle collisions. Next we should see exchanges between producers and consumers. And then these exchanges should lead to the emergence of money. It's pretty hard to say you have an economic explanation for things when you can't even explain money. People think of economics and money as going together.

Dr. Z: Does it explain any of these things now?

Sasha: Well, that's one problem we're having. So far we've seen a few producers, but the collider's not very good at consumers yet, and we haven't seen any money at all.

Bruce: Real science takes time. There's a difference between inventing something and having it work perfectly. You don't just throw a serious collider together overnight.

Brownie: But consumers? Like people? Isn't explaining where they came from a little outside the pale of economics?

Jim: Perhaps, but that's why we have Stu. He's a biologist. Quantum economics is interdisciplinary, you know.

Sasha: And Dr. Anderson, of course.

Brownie: Dr. Anderson? I don't believe Stu mentioned Dr. Anderson.

Sasha: Oh, he's a fisheries guy.

Brownie: Fisheries? What could that have to do with quantum economics?

Sasha: It's an adjacency. In interdisciplinary science, adjacent fields often contain important clues as to how things work. Plus exploring the space called "the adjacent possible" is an important way that biological organisms evolve.

Dr. Z: I see. Well, what have you done so far?

Jim: First we built all the machinery that you see here. Then we put fundamental economic particles in the collider, represented by numbers. They go in through the particle loader here (points out a device hooked to the particle collider).

Dr. Z: Really? What are economic particles?

Jim: The smallest abstractions you can imagine interacting to form the economy – economic quanta.

Bruce: Particles are like Lego™ blocks, which can be combined to form commodities. The Lego™ possibilities generator here (points out another device hooked to the collider) generates these commodity possibilities and feeds them into the collider.

Jim: (points to the collider itself) When a particle collides with a possibility that includes it, an agent, which can act on its own behalf, is created here in the collider. You might think of these agents as producers who can combine raw materials to produce something new. Like a producer, agents essentially buy their inputs and sell their output, which they do by exchanging either basic particles or combinations of these particles with one another through a process called "haggle."

Bruce: (rummages around in some papers) Let's see if we have a collision schematic here somewhere. Oh yes, here it is (shows Dr. Z the schematic). It's a bottom-up model, so you should either read it upside down, or start from the bottom and read up.

Dr. Z: What's this Economic Function Generator? I don't believe you've explained that yet.

Sasha: We're testing whether the agents exchange things based on what economists call production and utility functions – equations for how things are produced and consumed. If these equations describe how the economy really works, then money should emerge from agent exchanges that are based on them.

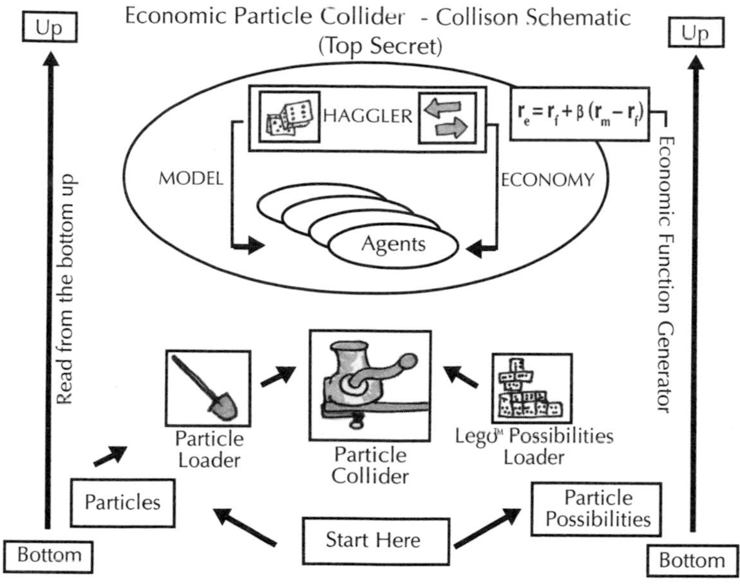

Bruce: (points to the function generator wired to the haggler) The functions go in right here. Jim was just working on the generator when you came in.

Jim: Yes, and now we're getting ready to do the hard work of science, testing these functions and looking for emergent money.

Dr. Z: Oh my, it's beginning to sound quite complex. How can you tell if you're seeing what you're looking for?

Jim: Oh, that's why we have the monitors here. (points out two monitors)

Bruce: Hmm ... (rummages around in his papers some more) I thought we also had an instrumentation diagram here somewhere. Yes, here it is. (proudly produces the diagram) Take a look at this – it might help.

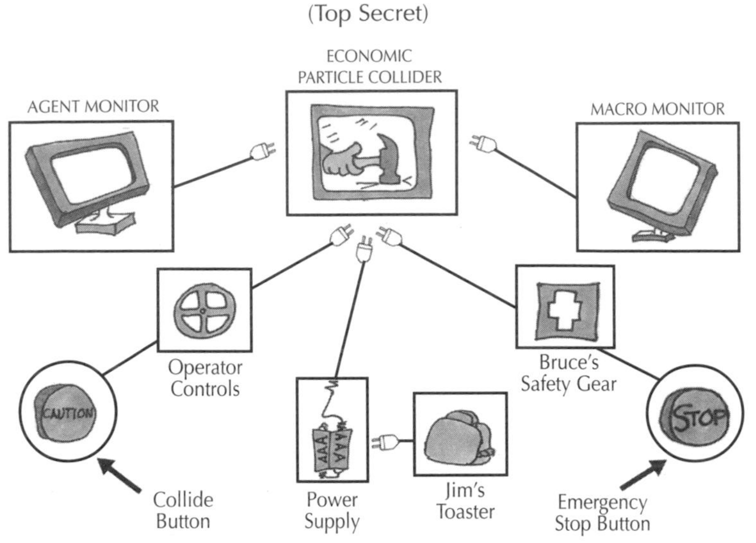

Bruce: Let me explain. It's pretty simple, really. Basically you look for measures of economy-wide activities on the macro monitor – things like power laws – and you look for measures of behavior at the agent level on the agent monitor.

Dr. Z: What are power laws?

Bruce: Equations of emergence! Power law patterns that emerge from particle interactions at the edge of chaos. We should see firms and currencies distributed in patterns like the ones we see in the real world. If we see these patterns, we have a bingo.

Sasha: For example here's a power law graph that shows approximately how firms are distributed by size in the real world (produces a graph).

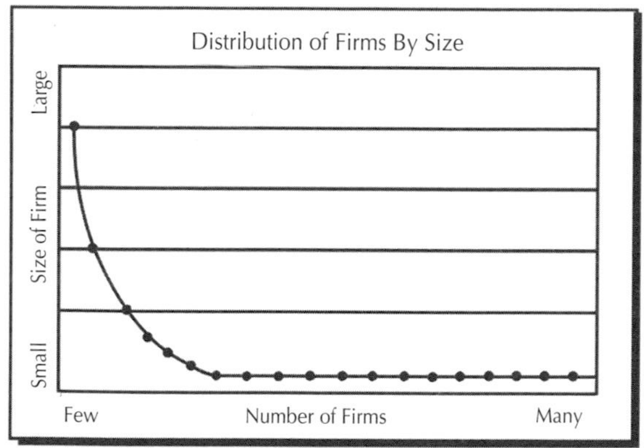

Sasha's Power Law

Dr. Z: Yes, that does look like the way firms are distributed, but what makes it a power law?

Sasha: Multiplying with exponents. A power law is just a relationship between two quantities in which one is proportional to a fixed power of the other.

Jim: Anyhow, to see power laws would be a partial bingo. But if we see patterns of individual behavior on the agent monitor like adaptation, co-evolution, and strategic economic behavior, and they result in institutions like complex firms, banks, and stock markets, like you see in the real world, then we will have a real bingo.

Sasha: The real bingo would be to see Schumpeterian gales on the macro monitor.

Bruce: Explaining gales will probably take years of work.

I mean we're talking here about predicting things like the Great Depression or the Dot Com Bomb.

Jim: Moreover, we're talking about modeling not just emergent values, but new products and ways of doing things that have never existed before.

Dr. Z: (losing interest in the instrumentation diagram and Schumpeterian gales) By the way, do you have debits and credits in this thing?

Sasha: Like in bookkeeping? Economists don't do bookkeeping.

Jim: Neither do scientists. This is a mathematical model, not a general ledger. Besides, I don't even know what those words mean – debits and credits.

Dr. Z: Neither do I – understand them, I mean – that's why I'm here. I'm looking for their true meaning.

Brownie: (changes the subject) So how does one collide the particles?

Jim: Oh, you just push the green button. In fact, we were just getting ready for the next trial run. Would you like to watch?

Dr. Z: (steps toward the collider enthusiastically) Oh yes!

Bruce: Whoa, stay away from that button, Professor! This is no work for amateurs. I need to get the emergency shutdown gear hooked up first.

Chapter 6

Tracking Down Quantum Economics

Meanwhile Thog had made his way to Mammoth Mountain. He didn't take along a spear on the plane, but he fashioned one quickly from local materials when he arrived. Mrs. Thog, as usual, had been quite right. It was no trouble at all to find the promised statue of a full-sized mammoth and, after looking it over and savoring a moment of nostalgia, he headed off in the snow with his spear.

There were people making strange tracks in the snow with sticks tied to their feet, so he made his way around to the other side of the mountain where any mammoth tracks would be less obscured.

Not my best spear, thrown together so quickly, he thought, as he walked along. But of course seeing a mammoth is pretty unlikely, anyhow.

The first thing he noticed were some rabbit tracks. "Confound these rabbits," he muttered, but he went ahead and speared a couple so he would have something to eat. Then he headed up the mountain with the rabbits over his shoulder.

Pretty soon he came to some strange-looking tracks in the snow. They apparently belonged to a two-legged creature with large webbed feet.

I may as well follow these for a while and see what this thing looks like, he thought.

No sooner had this thought crossed his mind than he heard a strange, wailing, high-pitched sound echoing through the mountains, "Yoodoolaadeehoo."

Well, at least I know what it sounds like, he thought, and if it keeps making noises like that, it shouldn't be very hard to find. In the old days tracking was an art!

Because of the obvious tracks in the snow and the strange noises the creature was making, Thog closed in on it in no time. Peering from behind a tree, he saw not a creature, but a cheerful man with wild hair in a bright purple parka trudging up the mountain. The man had webs attached to his feet and periodically he emitted a strange, ear-splitting noise.

Hmm ..., Thog thought, his footwear looks practical, but he sure makes a hullabaloo.

Over the eons, Thog has found that taking a win-win approach to new encounters is usually effective, so he stepped from behind his tree and said, "Hi, my name is Thog."

"Hi," the stranger replied, "mine is Stu Kauffman."

"What brings you to the mountain today, so ... ahh ... vocally?" Thog asked.

"Why, I came because it's here!"

Hmm ..., Thog thought, perhaps he's not so practical. "I see," he said.

"And what brings you?" Stu asked.

"Oh, I don't know, I was ... ahh ... I was just looking around to see if there were any mammoths," he replied a little sheepishly. "I used to hunt them, mastodon actually, but I suppose there are none left anymore."

"Yes, I think you'll have to dig for them if you're going to find any around here."

A good point, Thog thought. Perhaps he is practical after all. "Do you happen to like roasted rabbit?" he asked. "I have a couple we could cook up, and I know a recipe or two."

"As a matter of fact, I was just getting hungry. Let's gather some firewood," Stu said.

"Where are you from?" Stu asked when he and Thog were seated at the campfire.

"Right here," Thog said, drawing a map in the snow and pointing out his cave's location in the mountains outside Santa Fe.

"What a coincidence! I'm from Santa Fe, too."

"We just moved there ourselves," Thog explained, "you know – Wall Street problems."

"I'm sorry," Stu said, and then artfully changed the subject to avoid any embarrassment. "By the way, do you know Warren Miller?"

"No, I don't. Why do you ask?"

"Oh, he's a friend of mine who lived on rabbits while he was camping in the Sun Valley parking lot making ski movies. I thought because of the ski area, and your rabbits, that you might know him."

"I'm sorry I don't. I've never been to a ski area before."

Thog now found himself at a loss as to how to continue the conversation. He tried to think if he knew anyone Stu might know. "Speaking of rabbits, do you happen to know Leonardo? Some people call him Fibonacci."

"Why certainly," Stu exclaimed, "I know of him, at least. I don't believe I've ever heard him called Leonardo, but Fibonacci, of course, is the father of combinatoric mathematics – the one who made the famous rabbit computations that led to the field of statistics."

Well, this warmed the conversation right up, and after they had compared views on the Fibonacci series, combinatorial computations, statistics, and, of course, rabbits, Thog asked, "By the way, what do you do?"

"I'm a scientist."

"What type of scientist are you?"

"Originally I was a biologist, but now I'm what is called a complexity scientist."

"What's that?"

"Well," Stu said, and here he went on to give a fairly long response, covering the important contribution computers have made to science, how they led to the birth of computational experimentation and a new field called complexity science, and how complexity science is now helping people understand things like the co-evolution of species and possibly someday even the emergence of life from the edge of chaos.

Throughout this Thog sat spellbound, and when Stu had finished, thinking of Mrs. Thog's interest in books, he asked, "Is there anything one could read to learn more about this?"

To Thog's surprise, Stu rummaged around in his backpack and produced a book entitled *Investigations*. He handed it to Thog and said, "Here, take this. It might shed some light. I've just finished it."*

---

* He had literally just finished it – finished writing it, that is.

"Why, thank you very much."

Again Thog found himself at a social loss. Having received a gift, he wanted to reciprocate, but he was traveling light and all he had along was his spear. So he asked, "Would you consider accepting my spear as a gift? It was hastily built but it will do the job."

Stu, to be polite, said, "Certainly." Actually, he thought it might make a nice walking stick. "And how about you?" Stu asked. "What do you do?"

"Well, not much anymore," Thog said.

"What about before now? What did you do then?"

"Oh, our family was mostly what I believe you call bookkeepers, although we had a different name for it."

"By the way, you wouldn't happen to know anything about the true meaning of debits and credits, would you? A friend was just asking me about this the other day."

"Well, let's see, Mrs. Thog did invent them."

"Debits and credits? Really? And when might that have been?"

"Oh, I guess it was probably about 5,000 years ago or so. But during the 45,000 years before that, we had to invent some other things first, like models, money – that sort of thing."

"Oh my!" exclaimed Stu, who loves models and isn't that keen on debits and credits anyhow. "Tell me about your models."

"Well," Thog said, "modeling can become fairly involved ..." And he then proceeded with an explanation of the Thog family's modeling that rivaled in length Stu's description of the science of complex adaptive systems.

"And how about money?" Stu eventually asked.

"I should have said we discovered it instead of invented it," Thog apologized. "You see, after we invented money, we later learned that it was also what you might call invented in a number of other places as well. I didn't mean to seem immodest. It's just disappointing to think you invented something, only to learn that somebody else has already invented it."

"I understand," Stu said sympathetically. "That happens in science as well – more often than you might think."

"Yes, I suppose it must."

As he listened, Stu thought of Bruce, Jim, and Sasha back at PartEcon, struggling to get their model to produce money from particle interactions. "You know, Thog," he said, "right now some colleagues of mine in Santa Fe are trying to build a scientific model that explains how producers, consumers, and money came about in the first place. It's a new field of complexity science called quantum economics."

"Quantum economics, what a nice name," said Thog, who likes names.

"Since you're living near Santa Fe anyway, I believe my colleagues would be delighted if you'd consider working with them on their experiment."

"I would have to take that up with Mrs. Thog, of course. And there are the children's activities ..."

"Certainly," Stu said. "I'll understand if it doesn't work out."

At this point Thog noticed they had talked into the wee hours of the morning, not to mention having consumed two entire rabbits. "It's getting quite late," he suggested, "so what would you say to making a snow cave and camping here? We can walk down in the morning when there's more light."

The next morning was bright and sunny. Thog made up some snowshoes like Stu's. But before they started down the mountain, he said, "Stu, may I ask you a favor?"

"Certainly."

"Could you teach me to make that sound you were making when I first discovered you – the one you make just because the mountain is there?"

"Of course. It's called yodeling."

Then Thog, with an interesting new book in hand, and Stu, with a new spear serving as a walking stick, hiked down the mountain together, leaving webbed tracks in the new snow and yodeling joyfully, just because they and the mountain were there.

Chapter 7

Virtual Reality Mastodon Hunting

Upon his return from Mammoth Mountain, Thog was all aglow. He burst through the door, greeting Mrs. Thog and embracing her warmly.

Uh-oh, she thought, mammoths are supposed to be extinct. How could he possibly have found one? I can't imagine what else could explain his cheerfulness. But she kept this thought to herself, although as he hugged her she stood on tiptoes, looking over his shoulder to see what he might have dragged into the yard. "Did you find any mammoths, dear?" she asked.

"Just the statue, but I had a wonderful trip! And I can hardly wait to tell you about it."

"Well, I was just getting dinner. The children are out and about this evening, tidying up their commercial affairs before the recession begins in earnest."

Thog described the mountains, the rabbits, and meeting Stu Kauffman. He gave Mrs. Thog the new book Stu had given him, and mentioned Stu's invitation to work in Santa Fe on quantum economics.

"What a wonderful opportunity," Mrs. Thog said, delighted that Thog was showing interest in something other than mastodon hunting. "Perhaps the whole family could be helpful. I'm sure the children would enjoy it! You mentioned that Stu Kauffman emphasized computing's importance in this new quantum economics."

"Why, yes he did."

"Well," Mrs. Thog said, "while you were away, I read an interesting book on computing." She showed him Ray Kurzweil's *The Age of Spiritual Machines*. "Dr. Kurzweil has predicted that computers will be smarter than people by 2011."

"I'm not surprised," Thog rejoined. "All it would take is a little common sense – at least to be smarter than accountants these days. I suppose we'd better start learning more about these machines."

"Yes, I believe we should develop a win-win strategy with them as soon as possible," Mrs. Thog said. "In fact, I thought you might want to visit Dr. Kurzweil. He's really quite clever about computers."

"Well, dear, I'll get on the win-win problem with these computers first thing, and I'll go see Dr. Kurzweil immediately. After that I'll see Stu Kauffman and tell him we'd like to work with him on quantum economics."

Thog left the next morning for Boston and a visit with Dr. Kurzweil. (Confident of her persuasive powers over Thog, Mrs. Thog had arranged the trip as soon as she put down the Kurzweil book.)

In Dr. Kurzweil's waiting room, Thog encountered a life-sized wax figure, professorially attired, complete with a pipe.

Hmm ... Thog thought, I wonder if this is a model of someone extinct who didn't develop a win-win relationship with these smart new computers? Perhaps he is displayed here as a caution.

Thus sobered, Thog centered himself on his mission and waited anxiously for Dr. Kurzweil to appear. But when he did, Thog found him not the least bit intimidating, although he did have a mischievous twinkle in his eye.

"Hi, Thog," he said, "I'm Ray. Nice to meet you. I've heard a little bit about you from Mrs. Thog."

"Really?"

"She said you might like to go on a good mastodon hunt." ("Safely," Mrs. Thog had added, but Ray didn't mention this.)

This completely floored Thog. It took a moment for him to collect himself before he could stammer, "Why yes, mastodon hunting is my favorite thing in the world! But they're extinct now."

"Well," Ray said, chuckling, "I just thought perhaps you might enjoy hunting mastodon with me despite their extinction."

Dressed in a sport coat, Ray didn't look much like a mastodon hunter, and Thog didn't notice any spears or other hunting gear in the room, only computer equipment. On the other hand, it had been 11,000 years since Thog had been on a good hunt, so he replied, "What do you suggest we use for spears? I just gave mine away the other day."

Ray said, "We'll have to make some up when we get there."

"OK," Thog said. If this guy Ray can make a spear, that's

certainly a good start, he thought. "So where do you suggest we hunt and how do we get there?"

"Oh," Ray replied, "we're going to go in virtual reality."

"I don't believe I know where that is," Thog said.

As every good hunt begins with a thoughtful plan, Thog and Ray sat down and discussed their virtual reality mastodon hunt. And when they were satisfied with their plan, off they went.

The hunt was a spectacular success, Thog killed two, Ray one. Afterwards they spent some time looking at a few of Ray's inventions (including an earlier prototype of the Kurzweil converter).

"The converter is just a rudimentary example of artificial intelligence," Ray replied.

"Artificial intelligence?"

"Sure – computers that think like we do or better than we do. With the new computing developments, machine intelligence is growing very rapidly. Of course, an important key to intelligence is also knowing what not to compute."

"Ah yes," Thog said, "some accountants are still having trouble with that."

"Say, would you like to meet Ramona."

"Ramona?"

"Yes, she's one of my alter-egos in virtual reality."

"I don't suppose she hunts mastodon?"

"No, actually she prefers singing and dancing."

"Perhaps we should wait until Mrs. Thog is along.* She likes singing and dancing, and I really shouldn't take up too

---

* If you would like to meet Ramona, even though Thog didn't, you can find her at KurzweilAI.net along with a lot of interesting information about artificial intelligence.

much more of your time," Thog said, as politely as possible.
"Of course," Ray replied.
So Thog headed for home, suffused with the warm after-glow that follows a truly good mastodon hunt.

"They're bigger than I remembered."

Chapter 8

A Brush with Combinatoric Catastrophe

After Bruce Sawhill had assembled the emergency shutdown gear, Sasha Outkin reworked some economic equations at the whiteboard, and Jim Herriot made some final adjustments to the economic function generator. Then Bruce asked us all to stand behind a large Plexiglas shield, which we were more than happy to do.

Jim: Emergency stop gear check?

Bruce: Emergency stop gear ready.

Jim: All systems go?

Sasha: Affirmative, all go.

Jim: (pulls the lever on the particle loader) Particles in.

Bruce: Stable so far. OK to go with the possibilities.

Jim: (pulls the lever on the possibilities loader) Possibilities in!

Bruce: OK – activate the function generator.

Jim: (activates the function generator) Functions activated!

Bruce: Still stable – stand by to collide.

Jim: (hits the collide button) Colliding.

The particle collider sputtered, coughed a couple of times, and began to run haltingly.

Jim: Aha! It's finally unlocked.

Bruce: (watches the agent monitor) Hey, we're getting producers.

Sasha: (riveted to the macro monitor) No currencies yet.

Jim: (watches the macro monitor) No power laws, either.

Bruce: (listens to the collider) But it definitely sounds like we have something going on here.

Then the collider began to run faster and faster. The low hum turned to a loud whine, then a piercing wail, louder and louder. The collider turned red hot. The laboratory's red emergency lights began flashing. The warning siren went off and smoke poured from the collider, quickly filling the laboratory.

Bruce: (breaks the glass and hits the red button) Emergency Stop!! Whew, that was a close one! We were passing the edge of chaos!

Dr. Z: (breathless) Yes, but it was sooo exciting!

Bruce opened the window. As the last of the smoke cleared the room, we sat back down with the scientists. The mood was somber. Bruce suggested using carbon rods in the collider to absorb the runaway energy. Jim thought the problem might be in the possibilities loader. Sasha thought the economic function generator was causing the haggler to overheat. I don't think Dr. Z had a clue. And as for myself – well, with Dr. Z apparently distracted from debits and credits, I felt encouraged about getting out of there and back to New York. I was considering whether to use my laptop or my cell phone to book a quick return flight, when things took an entirely unexpected turn.

Stu Kauffman, whom I'd thought was away hiking in the mountains, sauntered through the door of the laboratory. Dressed in his hiking gear, he carried what looked to me like a spear. Other than the spear, he looked to be his usual dignified, rumpled, cheerful, professorial self. But what he said sounded not at all professorial. Perhaps I should let the converter explain:

Brownie: Hey, Stu. How are you?

Stu: Great, I see you made it. This must be your friend who's interested in debits and credits. (nods to Dr. Z)

Dr. Z: Very nice to meet you.

Stu: And the same. But hey, I saw the smoke. I thought perhaps the collider had gone combinatoric. Nobody was hurt, I hope?

Bruce: Nope. But it was a close one – very close!

Brownie: Say, I thought you were hiking.

Stu: I was. But I came back early because I met the most

interesting person and I was anxious to tell you about him. He just might be able to help with the collider. His name is Thog. He's a friend of Fibonacci's.

Bruce: Fibonacci? The father of statistics? I thought he was dead.

Stu: Yes, but Thog isn't. Plus, Thog invented money – well, his family did, I mean. Who should know better the architecture from which money emerged than its original discoverer?

Sasha: What kind of scientist is he?

Stu: Ahh ... well, he's not exactly a scientist. But he does have 50,000 years of practical experience.

Brownie: Are you sure you didn't get into the wrong mushrooms up there in the mountains?

Stu: Of course not. I'm a trained biologist.

Brownie: By the way, is that a spear you're carrying, or am I just imagining things?

Stu: Why yes, as a matter of fact it is – a gift from Thog. He's a hunter-gatherer. Actually, I'm using it as a walking stick. Perhaps I should explain.

Brownie: Perhaps you should.

Chapter 9

The Recruiting Mission

Stu pulled a chair up to the collider, put down his spear, and began to profess. I say profess, because like certain special college professors, Stu has an awesome vocabulary, which sounds wonderful, almost musical. His words captivate you and carry you along, even if you have no idea of what he's actually talking about.

I mostly heard a melodic blur of completely unintelligible stuff with scientific-sounding names. I did hear Stu say he was reminded of the fundamental constructs of nonlinear dynamics. And I noticed Bruce and Jim nodding in apparent understanding of how Stu thought this guy Thog might very well shed some light on the atomic structure of economics.

Dr. Z also listened to Stu with rapt attention. If I didn't know better, I might've thought she had an inkling of what he was talking about. But nonlinear dynamics – an accounting professor? Give me a break.

For my own part, I understood nothing except one big thing: my long-time friend, the once brilliant and esteemed Stuart Kauffman, scientist extraordinaire, had simply lost it. Conversing with a 50,000 year-old hunter-gatherer? Come on!

And I would have been on a plane headed back to New York and sanity, were it not for the fact that the troublesome topic of debits and credits managed to crop up.

In his discussion with Thog, apparently Stu, ever thoughtful, and mindful of my Dr. Z problem, had also asked Thog about debits and credits. Thog said that his wife had invented them herself. And needless to say, this did it for Dr. Z. She was locked and loaded, and with the Thogs in her sight reticule, her finger was quivering on the trigger.

Stu said he'd asked Thog to come to Santa Fe to help with the economic particle collider. "But he needed to check with Mrs. Thog, of course, and I believe I sensed reluctance. He's a little shy."

"For crying out loud, we can't just wait and see if he happens to show up!" Dr. Z exclaimed. "This is the opportunity of a lifetime! We have to seize it. We have to be proactive. We have to go get him. We have to recruit him – aggressively!"

"I think we should get some carbon rods in this thing before we go off recruiting," Bruce said. "Otherwise, we're liable to have a serious accident."

"Look," Dr. Z said, "why don't you guys stay here and get the carbon rods in the collider while Brownie and I go recruit the Thogs. Brownie's used to talking people into doing things even if they shouldn't. He used to be a CFO, you know."

The next thing I knew, I was at a Santa Fe outfitters purchasing a backpack that Dr. Z thought I needed, along with hiking boots and a safari shirt – pretty much a basic mountain recruiting outfit.

Chapter 10

The Thogs' Cave

The directions Stu gave us to the Thogs' cave were even more convoluted than those the day before to PartEcon. Plus this time it was uphill and we were on foot. Worse, I had offered to carry Dr. Z's book-stuffed pack. Oh well, I'm not the first guy on Wall Street to let his ego cloud his judgment, with unfortunate consequences.

Meanwhile, Dr. Z was skipping along with my pack. "This thing is really light," she said, rummaging through it. "Hey, where's the Kurzweil converter?"

"Oops," I said, "I must have left it back at the laboratory."

"You what?" Dr. Z exclaimed as she rolled her eyes in exasperation.

It was a long, hot hike in the sun. Dr. Z shared various observations about my organizational skills along the way, which made it seem even longer. Plus, her pack seemed to grow heavier with every step. I had begun to think we would never get there. It was nearly dark when we finally arrived at what was, indeed, a cave.

I'll admit I was somewhat incredulous. But I have to say, as caves go, it's quite nice. The view is more panoramic than from my Essex House apartment in New York, which is limited to Central Park.

I was looking over the cave and trying to catch my breath, but Dr. Z could sniff debits and credits in the air. She marched right up and knocked on the door.

Mrs. Thog answered. There really is a Mrs. Thog. And then there were the children – Thogette and Thog Junior – both smiling shyly. So we introduced ourselves.

Then Dr. Z said, "Dr. Stuart Kauffman from the Particle Economics Research Institute sent us to speak with your husband."

"Why, how thoughtful of Dr. Kauffman," Mrs. Thog said graciously. "Thog mentioned meeting him. He's the complexity scientist, I believe, the one working on quantum economics."

"Yes," Dr. Z said.

"Are you a quantum economist?" Mrs. Thog asked.

"Well, not exactly, but I'm a professor, and quantum decoherence – getting from yes and no to yes or no – is quite important in my work."

"Oh my, yes, we have found getting to yes or no extremely important as well," Mrs. Thog said. "Anyhow, I'm afraid Thog is away mastodon hunting at the moment. I don't expect him back until tomorrow. Sometimes these mastodon hunts go on and on, you know, although I have reason to believe that this one will be shorter than some. But you mustn't just stand outside – you really must come in. Please ..." And she showed us the way.

Mrs. Thog insisted we stay for dinner. Also overnight, as it was too late to hike back down the mountain in the dark. And there's really no arguing with Mrs. Thog. So we had a tour of the cave, which is very tastefully decorated, with some incredible paintings, a number of them by Thogette. We saw Thog's spear collection and Thogette's collection of miniature baskets, and models of some of Junior's inventions, the most intricate of which is an assembly line. Modeling, Mrs. Thog explained, is a family tradition.

Mrs. Thog and Dr. Z chatted about Mrs. Thog's book club and what they'd been reading recently. And Junior provided a knowledgeable description of a mastodon hunt, a complex undertaking compared with just chasing a few bulls and bears down a street in New York.

Mrs. Thog is quite the cook. We had a rabbit dish. She said it was her specialty, fashioned from a formulation by someone called Fibonacci. It was very tasty, finished with a piquant garnish. The mountain-greens salad was delicate, and the after-dinner coffee rich and aromatic.

The children were clearly comfortable around adults. Unlike some teenagers, they actually participated in the conversation. We chatted amiably over dinner and then retired to the living room and sat around a large stone fireplace where a fire burned cheerfully. In fact, the hunter-gatherer life didn't look all that bad to me.

But Dr. Z was in no mood to relax and chat. She simply had to get on track – to the truth of debits and credits.

"Mrs. Thog," she began, "I understand from Dr. Kauffman that you invented debits and credits? For my entire life I've been trying to understand their true meaning."

Mrs. Thog blushed and Thogette jumped in to answer for her mother, "Debits and credits? Oh yes, a long time ago. Of course, we don't use those names anymore. Daddy named them, he likes to name things, but it's true – they were originally Mom's idea. She came up with them shortly after she discovered zero. It was while she was working on Junior's first who by when."

"Of course, I've quite outgrown them now – debits and credits," Junior added.

"Well, mostly," Thogette said to annoy Junior.

"Did you know my Dad and Mom also invented the what by what?" Junior asked to change the subject from debits and credits and his first who by when.

"Who by which? What what?" Dr. Z asked, totally confused.

"The 'what <u>by</u> what.' But you don't write it like you say it. Let me show you," Thogette explained, carefully drawing "what <u>x</u> what" on a napkin. "The little x is an arithmetic idea."

"Junior, you're confusing Dr. Z," she added, when she'd finished her illustration.

"Oh I'm not confused at all," Dr. Z lied.

"Children, remember we have guests. For that matter, it's past your bedtimes," Mrs. Thog said. "We can discuss who x whens and what x whats in the morning."

Thogette whined, "Aw, Mom."

"Bedtime!" Mrs. Thog replied sternly.

At this the children trundled off to bed. Since we were tired from our hike, had full stomachs, and the warm fire made us drowsy, we took the opportunity to retire to our assigned guest rooms as well.

My head spun as I tried to get to sleep. Stock market chairmen don't hang around caves with the children of hunter-gatherers talking about who x whens and what x whats. How would this look in *The Wall Street Journal*? I would have been better off just to take the shot in Dr. Z's monograph. Nobody reads those things anyway.

Chapter 11

QUANTUM DECOHERENCE

Thog arrived shortly after breakfast. He looked to me – well – like a hunter-gatherer. It was quite a scene.

Mrs. Thog rushed to the door like a new bride. "Oh, here's Thog! Thog dear, we have company – visitors who are friends of Dr. Kauffman's."

This was followed by introductions all around.

"How is Stu?" Thog asked.

"Oh, he's fine," Dr. Z said. "And I believe he mentioned debits and – ..."

"So Thog, tell me about your mastodon hunt," I interrupted.

"Magnificent. A spectacular success. Ray Kurzweil is a most accomplished hunter."

"Ray Kurzweil?" I asked. "The scientist? He's a friend of mine. In fact, I have one of his computer inventions, a Kurzweil converter."

"Ah, yes. He showed me one. Wonderful invention, no question about it. Do you enjoy yours?"

"Well, yes, as a matter of fact – very much – it's quite helpful."

"When he can remember where he left it," Dr. Z muttered under her breath.

"And how did you find Ray's other computers, dear?" Mrs. Thog asked.

"You were quite right – they're absolutely wonderful. I'm certain that the opportunity to try things out in virtual reality will be an important tool of the future. But returning to your question about the hunt, Brownie. There was this huge mastodon. It was the last one we got – actually Ray is the one who got him – but you wouldn't believe how we found him – ..."

Mrs. Thog interrupted, "Dear, I'm sure everyone would love to hear the long story of your hunt, but Dr. Z has come to us with a pressing problem of a different sort, and I believe we should deal with it first."

"Why, yes, Dr. Z," Thog apologized. "How can we help you?"

"I'm searching for the true meaning of debits and credits. I understand your family invented them."

"I see. Stu mentioned he had a friend with such an interest."

"Perhaps you could tell me the story of how they came about."

"Why yes. We can do that. But, it's actually a little longer story than that of the hunt. Perhaps we should go inside and sit down where we'll be comfortable."

Mrs. Thog took up the story after everyone was comfortably seated, "Thog, dear, Dr. Z is a professor working with Dr. Kauffman on quantum economics, where she tells me getting to yes or no about things is quite important. Apparently her colleagues have a special name for it, different from ours. They call it quantum decoherence. Perhaps we should start the story of debits and credits with getting to yes or no."

"Ah yes," said Thog. "Getting to yes or no!"

As it turns out, Thog particularly likes getting to yes or no. In fact, Mrs. Thog sometimes complains he is a little too quick to do this. In fairness, however, she too is sometimes a little quick herself. Once when Thogette decided to date a young man from another tribe, Mrs. Thog got right to yes, while Thog took a little longer, but when Thog thought it a good idea to take eight-year-old Junior on a tiger hunt, Mrs. Thog got right to no.

"Decoherence is a nice term," Thog observed. "But we had a different name for this idea. We called it *getting to yes or no*, and we called the questions themselves *yes or nos*. And let me tell you, a mastodon hunt is no place for *yes and no* ambiguity. If you're dealing with an angry mastodon, you'd best get to yes or no about the situation – and I don't mean eventually. Forget perfection. Go for 'good enough.' For example, one time – ..."

"Dear, perhaps we should use a non-hunting example. Remember, Dr. Z is a professor."

"Ahh ... yes, of course, dear. Hmm ... let's see ..."

"How about counting?" Mrs. Thog suggested. "A number is a yes or no, of course. For example, are there six of us here or some other number? Yes or no? We've been counting for a very long time, and perhaps Dr. Z will find counting a somewhat more academic example than mastodon hunting."

"Come to think of it, I don't remember just when we started counting," Thog said.

"Nor do I, dear," Mrs. Thog said, "but perhaps that's not important to the example."

Although the Thogs couldn't remember just when they began counting, they remembered liking to count as long as 50,000 years ago.

Thog liked to count the number of people in his tribe, in case one got lost along the trail; how many people there were in an enemy tribe, in case he had to keep track of them in a battle; how many spears he had; and how many tigers or mastodon he killed on this hunt or that.

Mrs. Thog was a counter, too. She liked to count how many fruits and berries she gathered. And of course, from time to time she liked to double-check Thog's hunting reports for any exaggeration.

After explaining how much they liked counting, the Thogs' story turned from counting to nonquantitative observations.

"We didn't count everything, of course. There were other yes or nos besides counting," Thog said. "We didn't count the sharpness of our spears or the sweetness of our berries – you can generally tell if a spear is sharp or a berry is sour without counting – but these are yes-or-no questions just the same."

"Sometimes you have to live with yes and no for a while," Mrs. Thog added. "All of life does not occur with the urgency of a mastodon hunt, and when things are extraordinarily complex, sometimes all the questions involved aren't good enough for a yes-or-no decision at the same moment."

"Mrs. Thog is right," Thog said. "We've often found it best to take our yes or nos a step at a time. So Dr. Z," he concluded, "do you find our thinking about yes or nos consistent with your professional understanding of decoherence in general, as exemplified by counting?"

"Absolutely," said Dr. Z, whose work does involve some counting, although I knew that she'd never even heard of decoherence until Bruce mentioned it the day before.

"Well then, it sounds as though we are on the same page," he said.

"So far," Dr. Z affirmed.

Chapter 12

Carbon Rod Absorber Failure

While the Thogs were explaining hunter-gatherer decoherence, the PartEcon team was working on a physics problem of their own. Putting carbon rods in an economic model to avoid combinatoric catastrophes is not as easy as it sounds.

After they'd talked it over for a long time, Bruce, aided by Jim and Sasha, decided to build a carbon absorber for the collider, applying principles like those involved in a nuclear reactor, where carbon rods absorb the reactor's excess energy. Stu, meanwhile, had left for the mountains, where conditions were perfect for gathering exotic mushrooms.

"I sure hope this is gonna work," Bruce said as he tinkered with the absorber, his face black with carbon soot. "I've put in an awful lot of carbon."

"Well, we won't know until we try," Jim said, "but if I were you, I'd throw in a little more, just to be on the safe side."

"Good idea," Bruce said.

"Whoever would have thought that using economic functions would prove so disastrous?" Sasha asked wistfully.

"Economists are supposed to help prevent disasters, not cause them."

"OK," Bruce interrupted, standing up and wiping his hands on his hazard suit. "This is as good as I can get it. Let's set up the safety gear and get ready to collide."

But shortly after they hit the collide button, the alarms went off as the collider screamed out of control again. Thankfully, Bruce was quicker on the emergency stop button this time and there was a little less smoke.

"I don't know," Bruce said, dejected. "We used an awful lot of carbon and it didn't have much effect."

"How much carbon is it going to take?" Sasha asked. (He sometimes thinks in terms of supply and demand.) "Do you suppose we can even get enough?"

"If you ask me," Bruce said, "it's gonna take something other than carbon to get this baby under control."

"The economic functions may be overheating the haggler," Sasha observed. "Maybe there's something fundamentally wrong with using economic functions in the first place."

"You know, I think you're right," Jim said. "The carbon absorber and function generator are too high up in the scheme of things for a truly atomic-level, bottom-up model. We got carried away and reverted to the old top-down approach to problem-solving. We need to remember that we're complexity scientists and focus on the particles and agents instead."

"Let's clean up this mess, get rid of the carbon absorber, get rid of the economic function generator, and go back to square one," Bruce suggested. "I think it's time to review our basic modeling approach."

Jim and Sasha nodded in solemn agreement.

"I'm gonna put the absorber in the hazardous waste container," Bruce said, unplugging the absorber.

"I'll put the function generator in there, too," Sasha said.

"By the way, I wonder how Brownie and Dr. Z are doing?" Jim asked. "Aren't they supposed to be recruiting Thog?"

"Maybe they got lost in the mountains somewhere," Bruce said. "It's easy to get off track up there."

"Should we go look for them?" Sasha asked.

"Maybe, but I think we should go look for Stu first," Jim said. "We need to review our scientific approach from square one with him."

Chapter 13

Standards and Records

Back in the cave, Mrs. Thog turned from the yes-or-no aspects of nonquantitative observations back to the story of counting:

"If there is a lot of what you're counting, the number of yes or nos involved can add up pretty fast," she said.

"For example," Thogette offered, "Mom used to just hate counting individual berries. You should have heard her complain."

"Dear?" Mrs. Thog said, looking quizzically at Thogette.

"Mrs. Thog almost never complains," Thog added, jumping to her defense. "Counting berries was very tedious work."

"As I was about to say," Thogette huffed, "this is when Mom came up with the idea of counting basketfuls instead of individual berries."

"It was a capital idea!" Thog said. "It made counting much simpler and in no time led to using other things, like stones, for weighing things."

"And your foot for measuring distances, Dad – remember that?" Junior piped in.

The Thogs explained how the practice of using physical objects to represent what they were measuring grew. The objects stood for ideas everyone understood, and they decided to call an object representing such an idea a *standard*. Later on they used symbols instead of objects for the same purpose, and they called these "standards" as well.

"Actually, Daddy named them," Thogette said.

Junior said, "A standard is also important because it's a record, a way of keeping track of a past notion for future reference."

"Oh my yes," Dr. Z interrupted, "standards are very important in accounting or in any measurement, for that matter."

"Speaking of standards," Thog mused, "do you remember Chief Lion Ring?"*

"How could I forget?" Mrs. Thog replied.

"Now <u>there's</u> a story. When Mrs. Thog came up with the basket idea, Chief Lion Ring liked it a lot. So he decided there should be a standard basket for use by the entire tribe. This way, when we were dividing things up, everyone had the same idea of how much a basket represented. And, he decided to display the official basket outside his cave, so everyone could check their own baskets against his standard."

"But then Chief Lion Ring got a little carried away," Mrs. Thog said. "And the next thing you know, there was a huge collection of standards in front of his cave – baskets, stones, you name it. Chief Lion Ring wanted a standard for everything, and before long he required that the entire tribe attend regular meetings to be sure his standards were what he called 'generally accepted.'"

---

* Chief Lion Ring was a hunter-gatherer who stood off a ring of angry lions.

"Yes," Thog added. "Pretty soon we were spending more time arguing about general acceptance than hunting and gathering, and this became a problem. Finally old Lion Ring decided to keep his standards hidden from public view and bring them out only to adjudicate disputes and teach the children. This way, at least those of us not directly involved in the debates were able to return to hunting and gathering."

Thogette picked up the story. "Then Chief Lion Ring got so confused by all the stuff in his cave that he got the standards all mixed up. Nobody had any idea of what they all were, and before you know it, no one in the tribe could tell how much anything was anymore – quantitatively speaking, of course."

"Oh, I'm sure he meant well," Mrs. Thog interjected. "I think he just let things become too complicated and then lost track of them."

Chapter 14

Thogian Modeling

After the Lion Ring interlude, Thog explained that he was not one of the tribal elders – not elder material – nor was Mrs. Thog. So while Chief Lion Ring and the elders were in his cave debating standards, the Thogs were out hunting and gathering.

In his work, Thog spent a fair amount of time thinking about where tigers and mastodon might be found and how best to hunt them. And in her work, Mrs. Thog thought quite a bit about where best to gather her fruits and berries and how best to do it.

At dinner one night Thog and Mrs. Thog each expressed curiosity about where the other planned to spend the following day. In the course of their discussion, they invented a very helpful tool: a simplified picture of where they planned to go. Thog thought they should call this tool a *map*.

They used the same method to invent maps that had yielded up numbers and counting. For numbers, they left out nearly all details about what they were counting and retained only a general description. This way they reduced important questions about manyness and sequence to a yes or no, permitting a number like "three" to apply equally to tigers, spears, and baskets of berries.

Similarly, when they invented maps they omitted extraneous details about the natural terrain. The trail was a line scratched in the dirt, and the location of a few dangerous spots along the trail, as well as particular landmarks and other features, were identified with similar marks. This provided a yes-or-no record of where things were: yes, this is the right trail, no, this is not the right mountain, and so forth.

Mrs. Thog thought they should name not only maps but also locations on maps – their cave's location, for instance – and Thog suggested they call such a location an *address*.

With maps and addresses invented and named, the Thogs enjoyed new prosperity. Thog could keep track of where the best hunting spots were and could find them readily with their addresses, and Mrs. Thog could keep a nice record of the best gathering spots.

Dr. Z asked the Thogs if they remembered when it was that they'd invented maps and addresses. The Thogs all looked at each other. They didn't. But here's an incident they did recall:

"Dad," Junior asked one evening, "can I go on a tiger hunt with you?"

"Absolutely not!" Mrs. Thog interjected. "You're far too young."

"Aw, c'mon, Mom," Junior whined.

"Junior," Thogette taunted, "you shouldn't ask a yes-or-no question if you can't take no for an answer."

Junior glowered at her.

"Your mother is right," Thog added, "you're still too small to carry a spear."

I'd better take this yes-or-no stuff a step at a time, Junior thought, so he said, "How about putting aside the question of size, and simply getting to yes or no about the question of my having a spear?"

"A spear," Thog asked incredulously, "whatever for?"

"For practice. You do plan on taking me tiger hunting eventually, don't you?"

"Of course – someday."

"You wouldn't expect me to go without practicing, would you?"

"Of course not."

"Well, then why not make me a smaller spear right now – one my size? You know, like you made the mountain on the map smaller than it really is? But I'd like my spear to be exactly the same as yours, just smaller, so there won't be any doubt about whether it's really a spear."

"Uhh … I think Junior has a point here," Thog admitted.

"Hey, Mom," Thogette interrupted, "you could make me some smaller baskets so I can practice gathering, too."

"Why, of course," Mrs. Thog said.

"What shall we call these little things, Daddy?" Thogette asked.

"Hmm …" Thog replied. "They are very much like maps. I suppose we could call them … ahh … something similar … how about *models*?"

"What a nice choice," Mrs. Thog said. "The alliteration emphasizes their relationship."

Chapter 15

Agent-Based Modeling

In Santa Fe the PartEcon team was studying a map of their own, trying to find out where Stu was gathering exotic mushrooms. It took a while, but eventually they tracked him down.

"The collider went combinatoric again despite the absorber," Jim explained.

"We think we should start from the beginning and review our basic modeling approach," Sasha said, "just to be rigorous."

"Then I guess we'd better go back to the laboratory," Stu replied.

When they had gathered in the lab again, Stu began, "Well, modeling is clearly the thing to be doing. I don't know any credible scientists who disagree with my friend John Holland,* who says that all of science is based on the construction of models."

"So at least we're being scientific," Sasha said, "even if we aren't making much progress."

Bruce, the history buff, said, "Modeling began with the first maps, and mankind went on to model using gods and

---

* A well-known complexity scientist.

rule-bound sacrifices, then mechanisms like gates, pumps, and wheels, and finally complex abstractions."

"Thanks to computing," Jim added.

"Yes," Bruce continued. "Until a hundred years ago, scientific models were still restricted to systems with only a few components. For example, Newton explained gravity in terms of an apple falling from a tree or a planet orbiting around the sun. Newtonian models included initial conditions and universal physical laws, with equations that scientists could solve by hand – like where a fired projectile might land. And Newton, being a considerate guy, also invented the calculus so you could solve those self-same nifty equations."

"But things like the weather and the economy involve problems that are too complex to compute by hand," Sasha said.

"Which led to the popularity of what another of my old colleagues, Murray Gell-Mann* calls computational experimentation," Stu said.

"And when it comes to computational experimentation, we're state of the art," Jim said. "The collider is an agent-based model. Agent-based models have been successful for everything from interdicting terrorists, optimizing military battlefield tactics and untangling traffic jams, to predicting fisheries biomass and sorting out airline maintenance complexities. So an agent-based model should do for explaining how the economy works as well."

"Yes," Stu said. "I believe we're on the right track using agent-based modeling."

---

* A physicist and Nobel laureate.

After working themselves up like this, they all nodded in sober affirmation.

"But maybe we're missing something in the way our agents interact," Sasha said. "After all, an agent faces the dilemma that the outcome of an interaction depends on the behavior of another agent."

"Ahh. . .that's the Prisoner's Dilemma, also called the Prisoner's Paradox, a key discovery in game theory, first described by Flood and Dresher in 1950," Bruce said. "My favorite example is where two strangers at the scene of a crime are arrested as suspects and jailed in separate cells where they can't communicate. The authorities realize they don't have enough evidence to convict either on the main charge, although a lesser charge will get both sentenced to a year in jail. But, hoping for a more newsworthy result, the prosecutor approaches each prisoner with the same deal: If you testify against the other, you can go free and he will get twenty years on the main charge, but if you don't and he testifies against you, you will get twenty years and he will go free."

"Of course they both rat on one another," Jim added. "But I prefer the Red Queen example,* the coevolutionary arms race between predator and prey, where all species keep changing and changing their genotypes indefinitely in a never-ending race just to sustain themselves. It's more dynamic than a couple of guys sitting around a jail cell for twenty years after just one interaction."

"Regardless of your favorite example, the Paradox is not only important in game theory but in psychology, sociology,

---

*Named after the Red Queen in Lewis Carrol's *Through the Looking Glass.*

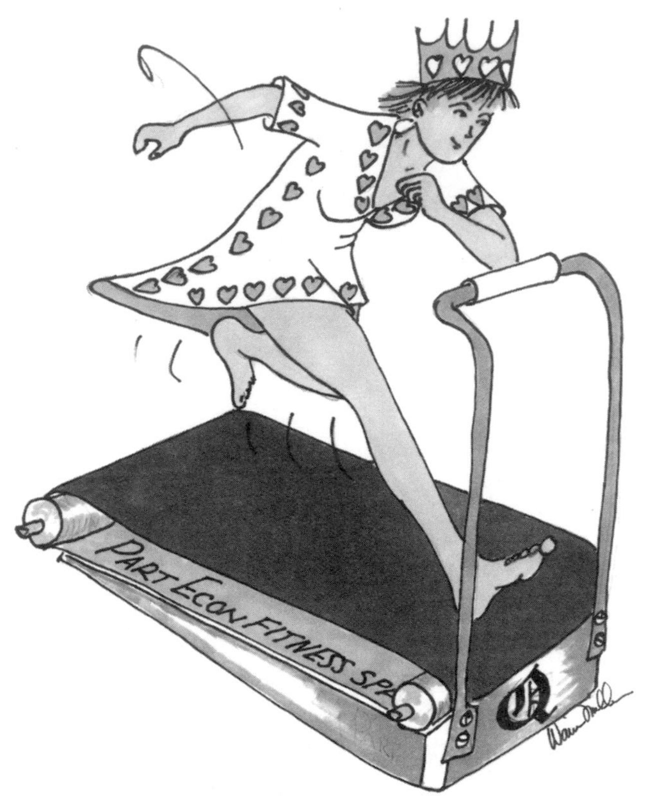

"It takes all the running you can do to keep in the same place," the Red Queen panted.

law, and many other fields as well," Stu added. "In fact, in biology a number of my colleagues consider it the dominant framework for the evolution of the species."

"Hey, do you remember the contests that John Holland and Robert Axelrod held at the University of Michigan?" Sasha said. "They tested all those mathematical strategies to see which could overcome the Paradox in an iterated game."

"I sure do," Bruce said. "There were scads of strategies over the years, conceived by any number of smart people – very smart people – and the only successful strategy thus far has been the simple little win-win program the Canadians came up with, called 'Tit for Tat.'"

"That's right," Jim said. "Four lines of code, and it eventually overcomes the Paradox every time. Start out by cooperating, and abandon cooperation only <u>after</u> the other guy does."

"Hey, guys!" Bruce exclaimed. "I've got an idea. Let's give the agents the Tit for Tat code. Not only does it eventually work every time in the face of the Paradox, there's experimental evidence that indicates the agents themselves will evolve Tit for Tat, or a strategy very much like it, from random trial and error. That is if they keep at it for long enough."

"It would sure save some computing," Jim said, "and with all the evidence that it will likely evolve anyway, I think we should go ahead and give Tit for Tat to the agents."

"I'll pull up the papers on the experiments," Sasha said, getting excited.

"I think having the agents use Tit for Tat is a good move," Stu said.

"OK," Jim said, "we'll give it a shot – trial and error, the essence of science."

"Ah yes," Bruce said, still in an historical mood, "I suppose Thales the Greek said something along those very lines in 600 BC when he conceived the scientific method. It's the same idea really – trial and error – mathematically measured, of course."

On this note, Stu went back to gathering his mushrooms while Jim worked on the four new lines of Tit for Tat code for the agents, and Bruce and Sasha checked over the safety gear for the next trial run – just in case.

Chapter 16

The Take or Trade Problem

Thog explained that, thanks to maps, Mrs. Thog became a very accomplished berry gatherer, which allowed her to make his favorite dessert as often as twice a week, whereas before maps he was lucky to get it once a month.

"And you really haven't lived until you've tasted her recipe," he added.

When Thog finished discussing desserts, Mrs. Thog went on to explain that maps also enabled Thog to travel more widely on his hunting expeditions. And it was on one of these trips that he discovered another tribe – the Deltas.*

With his counting, measuring, and modeling skills, Thog was well equipped to consider how the Deltas were different from his tribe, so he stayed carefully concealed, hoping not to attract their attention. They appeared to use a slightly better hunting model than his – at least they were getting more tigers than he was. On the other hand, they apparently had no mastodon – a shame!

The Deltas also used an unfamiliar model for getting what he heard them call "fish." Thog wasn't too sure if he'd like

---

* The Deltas were named for the river delta where they lived.

eating fish – he's a hunter, after all – but he knew that Mrs. Thog liked a little variety in her life. The things called fish might appeal to her. Plus the Deltas had some very nice beads that he knew she'd like.

After surreptitiously taking in the scene, Thog decided to go home and talk with Mrs. Thog about what he'd observed. En route, he saw Chief Lion Ring out in front of his cave, enjoying a break from the standards debates, and to be polite Thog stopped to chat; he mentioned seeing the Deltas.

At dinner, after hearing Thog's story, Mrs. Thog said, "Their beads sound lovely, and the fish might be a nice change from tiger and mastodon."

Thog looked crestfallen.

"Why, I meant for an occasional change," she added quickly, sensing his wounded hunter's pride, "not as a regular diet."

"The problem is we don't know much about the Deltas, let alone their fish," he said. "So I'm uncertain how my first interaction with them will turn out."

"What are the alternatives?"

"I spoke with Chief Lion Ring and he thinks we should just kill the Deltas and take their stuff – the usual."

"I should think Chief Lion Ring has enough worries over his standards problems without declaring a war to boot."

"Worse," Thog added, "the Deltas looked to me like good hunters. They might kill us, instead."

"It would be hard to learn how they catch their fish if you kill them."

"There is that," he said. "I wonder if they'd enjoy mastodon? They don't appear to have any. We could offer them some in exchange for some fish."

"I should think they might like a change from their fish."

"I'm really stumped about what to do," Thog said, scratching his head. "This is a regular yes-and-no dilemma."

"Well, I guess you'll just have to do the best you can to explore it, carefully of course. And while you're considering how to go about it, you might also think about what we should call this particular problem."

"Let's see," said Thog, relieved by a distraction from the prickly dilemma. "I suppose we could call it the *take or trade* problem. That's the essence of it, really."

"What a lovely name! When this sort of situation comes up again, we'll know just what to call it."

By the next morning Thog had come up with a strategy: he decided to break down his dealings with the Deltas into little yes-or-no decisions until he could learn more about the situation. He would test the results carefully, one step at a time.

He would wait until an individual Delta appeared by himself, one who looked bright and not too ferocious. If the Delta acted friendly, Thog would take several more careful little yes-or-no steps, depending on the circumstances. But the goal in the end was to offer him some mastodon and, he hoped, exchange it for some fish.

If the Delta turned out to be unfriendly, both of them would either back down or Thog would have to kill him. So he would prepare for this eventuality.

"It sounds like an excellent strategy," Mrs. Thog said when he told her over breakfast. "I suppose we should have a name for it."

"Since the essence of it is attempting to cooperate so that both traders win, perhaps we should call this strategy a *win-win*."

"Yes, a very nice name," Mrs. Thog said. "And in contrast to Chief Lion Ring's plan, at least you and the Delta won't need to try and kill one another."

"Yes," Thog said, "there may be more advantages to these win-win strategies than just their possibilities in trade."

Chapter 17

The Trial and Error Method

We took a short dinner break after hearing about Deltas and win-wins. The fish piqued my interest; as a fisherman myself, I wondered: nets or lines? how deep? which phase of the moon? – the usual stuff. But Thog didn't seem much interested in how the Deltas caught their fish, so I didn't pursue it. And Dr. Z had a full head of steam up – what with yes or nos, standards of measure, modeling, and the take or trade problem under her belt – so she kept after the Thogs to continue their story:

Chief Lion Ring remained too enmeshed in standards debates to declare war, which gave Thog a peacetime opportunity to try out his win-win strategy on the Deltas.

But, as with many well-planned strategies, it didn't work out – at least not at first.

Thog sought out a Delta who seemed intelligent and not too bellicose, and engaged him in conversation. They had a friendly chat, and taking things a step at a time they navigated through a number of little yes or nos. But then they hit a deal breaker.

"I was thinking that you might enjoy mastodon – you know, for a little variety in your diet," Thog said. "Mrs.

Thog and I are especially fond of it. In fact, to come to the point, I was thinking that you might like to trade some mastodon for some fish."

"I don't think so," the Delta countered.

"Really?" Thog said. "Would it be rude to inquire why not?"

"Not at all. My wife and I have no idea how to prepare mastodon."

So Thog returned home empty-handed, his first attempt to implement the win-win strategy unsuccessful.

When he told Mrs. Thog that the Delta didn't want to trade because he didn't know how to cook mastodon, she said, "Perhaps you should have offered him one of my recipes."

Thog looked crestfallen. "I didn't think of that."

"Maybe it's not too late."

Which is how it came to pass that Thog and Mrs. Thog returned together the next day to engage the Delta and his wife in a further negotiation. And this time they got to yes. In fact, in no time flat the ladies were happily comparing recipes, and Thog not only got fish but some beads that particularly appealed to Mrs. Thog.

So the Thogs returned home with their bounty in a jovial mood. "There's nothing like a recipe for facilitating trade," Thog said.

"Why yes," Mrs. Thog agreed. "A recipe is about combining several things to make something more pleasant than the mere sum of its parts."

"I guess it all goes to show the importance of learning from experience," Thog said.

"Yes, dear. Perhaps this approach of learning from experience is sufficiently general that we should give it a name."

"Ahh... yes, a name. What shall we call it? How about the *trial and error method*? That's the essence of it, really – you know, try out a measurable idea and adjust it for any mistakes."

"A lovely name," she said. "It works nicely for improving recipes and I'm sure it will prove to be an important methodology for other things as well."

It was getting pretty late by the time we finished this episode. Mrs. Thog sent the children off to bed, Thog yawned a magnificent yawn, and we all retired for the night.

Chapter 18

A Rough Collider Run

The economic functions and carbon had made a mess of the laboratory, and it took the PartEcon team the balance of the afternoon to clean it up, so it wasn't until next morning that they convened to test the effect that Tit for Tat code might have on the emergence of producers, consumers, money, and whatnot. (Stu was absent again; this time he had to present an academic paper at a biology conference in Santa Fe.) After Jim fed the four new lines of code to the agents and warmed the collider up in its standby mode, they hit the collide button.

And they had a pleasant surprise: it didn't go combinatoric! The collider ran, wheezing and snorting erratically and making a variety of other unusual noises, none of which were very reassuring. But they were able to monitor its progress without a catastrophe.

"It's not completely clear what we have here," Sasha said. "But the collider sure seems to work better without all those functions."

"Maybe the agents are just getting used to the new code," Bruce suggested.

"There's only four lines of it," Jim said. "It's sure taking long enough."

"Let's keep watching the monitors and see what happens," Sasha said.

Eventually both producers and products appeared on the agent monitor– agents combining particles just as if the particles were Lego™ blocks. Unfortunately this occurred only after they had watched the collider churn along and then gasp alarmingly. And Sasha, thinking it about to die, had thrown in some consumers to help the process along. "Not enough consumers for trading to occur," he explained.

With the input of extra consumers, the collider ran a little better, although it continued to belch smoke and make occasional obnoxious noises.

"Still no money," Sasha said. Frustrated, he sprinkled in some money. This smoothed out the operation a little, but still the collider ran rough.

"It's more fun than watching a catastrophe," Bruce said.

"Yes, but it's not very scientific to be adding the consumers and the money from the top down. I guess my economics habits overwhelmed my physics training," Sasha said. "For economics to become a real science, we're going to have to figure out how to make things work without cheating."

"I always thought of scientific cheating as relative," Jim said. "Sometimes it's considered scientific to cheat a little while you're figuring out how to make things work without cheating."

"Less so in physics than in economics," Sasha replied.

"I'm afraid he's right," Bruce added.

This remark provoked a lengthy discussion about scientific cheating – the various precedents and rationalizations for it – but as time wore on and prospects for any further collider results grew dim, they decided to turn off the machine and gather around the whiteboard to brainstorm.

"One problem with Tit for Tat is that an agent can't measure whether a possibility is a win," Bruce said. "It's limited to thinking of a win as getting a particle it needs or giving up one it doesn't. From an agent's perspective, all the particles are equal. But they aren't equal in the real economy. When an agent haggles, it needs a way to consider particle differences in deciding whether to complete an exchange."

"How can an agent do that before the collider has produced money with which to measure the particles?" Jim asked.

"This is the problem of which came first, the agent or the money?" Sasha said. "It's like – how do you say in America? – the chicken or the egg, no?"

"An agent needs some kind of record of what it knows – to help it decide how to haggle," Jim mused.

"Ray Kurzweil likes to say that DNA is life's basic recordkeeping system," Bruce said, "providing a record of achievement from one generation to the next and permitting progress by avoiding an endless loop of repeated mistakes."

"Then maybe we should try genetic algorithms," Sasha said.

"Yeah, we could measure exactly how to replicate each agent," Jim said, "and if agents of a particular genetic species were growing in number or dying off, we could at least see that. It would be sort of a survival-of-the-fittest kind of thing."

"Sure, but it would be a lot better if an agent could measure whether it's prospering or failing as it goes along – you know, before it's dead," Bruce said. "An agent needs to haggle before it's gonzo."

"Well, DNA is just ordered binary pairs," Sasha said. "Maybe what we need here is a record involving ordered binary pairs that lets an agent measure how it is doing as it goes along."

"Now that sounds right!" Jim exclaimed. "I think that's exactly what we need to do. Let's invent it!"

So they set about inventing a record for the agents in the collider that would enable one agent to haggle with another, and each agent in a potential exchange to measure and decide for itself whether that exchange looked like a win. And with Sasha at the whiteboard, the sigmas and deltas literally flew as the three scientists explored the mathematical possibilities.

Chapter 19

Mrs. Thog's Tally Sticks

Back in the cave, the Thogs explained that word about the win-win benefits of exchanging things got around, and soon they had a flourishing trade with the Deltas. But trade was not without problems.

One evening Thog complained to Mrs. Thog: "The other day, I lugged four stones of mastodon meat up to the Deltas. I planned to trade it for four stones of fish, but they only had two stones on hand. So I ended up carrying two stones of my own mastodon back home. And the worst of it is, they wanted all the mastodon meat. I'm sure that by now they've caught two more stones of fish up there, while my two stones of mastodon are spoiling down here. It's a timing problem, really."

"To save all these trips up and down the trail, perhaps you could find some way to start a transaction now and finish it later," Mrs. Thog said.

"I'll say!"

"Perhaps a record would be helpful. I find one helpful in my berry picking."

"Maybe I'd better have a look at your berry record, dear."

Mrs. Thog brought him a stick and explained, "I notch a

stick like this for each basket of berries I pick. Perhaps you could notch a stick for the number of stones of fish due you. If you had one today you could have left your mastodon meat with the Deltas and picked up the two stones of fish they owe you on your next trip. The stick would remind both you and the Delta of what's owing, and the mastodon wouldn't be spoiling."

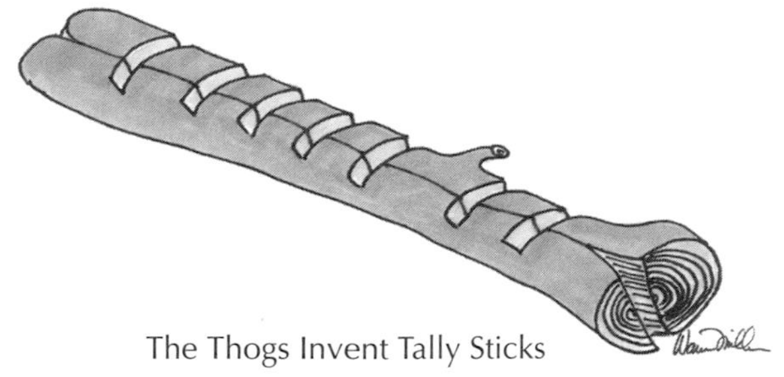

The Thogs Invent Tally Sticks

"What a capital idea!" Thog exclaimed. "In fact, after I notched the stick I could split it into two identical halves that each of us could keep. When it comes time to settle up, he'd have a record and so would I – a pair of records."

"Why, that's a marvelous improvement over a single stick!" she said. "If you suspect a Delta of cheating with his notches, you can put the two halves of the original stick together and see if any of the original notches have been tampered with."

So this is how the Thogs invented what they decided to call *tally sticks*. These matched pairs of sticks – split from a notched original – were soon in widespread use throughout what we now know as Africa, China, Europe, the Pacific, and North America.

"Oh my!" Dr. Z said. "Not only did you invent tally sticks, but you also invented what we now call a 'contract' as well as 'credit.' A contract is just a measurable agreement, and credit allows a transaction to be started now and completed later. In fact, the Chinese written symbol for the word 'contract' still includes a notched stick and knife, and the Arab verb root 'farada' still means both 'to make a notch' and 'to assign a contract share.'"

"My goodness," Mrs. Thog said, "and we were just trying to save an extra trip down the trail lugging some mastodon!"

"Oh, contracts are the basis of all transactions," Dr. Z gushed. And once she got herself worked up, she had a virtual epiphany and carried on about contracts and credit right through lunch.

Chapter 20

Matrices and Fitness Landscapes

While we were busy learning about tally sticks, the PartEcon team had convened in the laboratory. Their measurement work had kept them up late the night before. Sasha's hand eventually cramped, so Jim relieved him on the whiteboard. Then Bruce relieved Jim, and by the wee hours they still hadn't come up with a record that involved ordered pairs for the agents to use in haggle. Every possibility they investigated led to a mathematical contradiction, and when writer's cramp eventually got the better of them all, they finally gave up for the night.

They were on their third cup of coffee when Stu stopped in to see how things were coming along and heard their story.

"OK, maybe we should go through this one more time from the beginning." (Stu likes to review.)

"Well," Sasha said, "we're looking for something like DNA consisting of ordered pairs."

"Yes," Bruce said, "which should enable us to measure agents in a traditional state space." (Physicists like state spaces.)

"A state space," Sasha said, thinking out loud, "is just a map of the measurement possibilities for a system of interacting particles."

"Speaking of maps and interacting particles," Bruce said, "at this point I'd settle for just about any map in the collider – even if it's just something like longitude x latitude, forget altitude for now." (Like the Thogs, scientists write this with a little "x," but say "by.")

"At the very minimum, a map for the agents will have to be a something x something," Jim replied.

"It'll have to be a something x something that expands as the collider runs," Bruce said. "Each agent can't start with everything x everything in the beginning."

"That's right," Jim said, "that would be infinite – uncomputable."

"As the map expands, it would be nice if agent population x the passage of time would eventually emerge. This would yield a simple fitness landscape," Stu said.

(Biologists like fitness landscapes, often conceived of as ranges of mountains and valleys through which an evolving population climbs to reach a local optimum until a mutation occurs permitting it to reach a higher local optimum. A landscape with many local peaks surrounded by deep valleys is called "rugged.")

"A rugged landscape with more dimensions would be even better and more realistic," Stu continued.

"Ah yes, your bromine fog scenario," Bruce said.

"Bromine?" Sasha asked.

"Imagine a rugged fitness landscape in which the valleys are filled with a poison bromine fog. When a species descends too low from a prior local optimum in search of a new one, they become extinct," Stu said.

"Why bromine?" Jim asked.

"Well almost any poison fog would serve," Stu replied, "as long as the molecules were large enough to be dispersed as a fog, but bromine is a nice example because of its dark red color and noxious odor."

"Plus the red is reminiscent of the Red Queen problem we were discussing earlier," Bruce suggested.

"If the vapor level keeps rising, we're going to have to move camp to a higher altitude."

"I guess the main idea here is that we need something we could graph," Sasha interjected. "Many economists are happy if they can graph something – anything. It would be helpful for communicating with them."

"But remember, even a fitness landscape will require an emergent binary measure that is common among the agents," Jim said. "We need to be able to compare one agent with another to see if they're alive or dead, or growing or dwindling, or doing whatever we end up being able to measure."

"I know, I know," Sasha said, "something like money."

"I think we're going in a circle again, just like last night," Jim said.

"Well," Bruce said, "we need a something x something, and whatever it turns out to be it'll be a matrix – a grid of possibilities. As I recall, John Sylvester named the notion in 1848 from the Latin word for 'womb.' He became famous because matrices led to linear algebra, physics, computing, nonlinear dynamics and, of course, pretty much what we're trying to do here at PartEcon."

"I'm more interested in making economics scientific," Sasha said, "forget famous."

"So I guess we'll have to do a little homework – brush up on our matrix algebra," Jim said. "Maybe we're missing something algebraic – a wrong vector or something."*

"We may be missing something very basic and more important," Stu mused. "Perhaps we should go back to the particles and break them down into the most basic things possible: bits. Perhaps we should be using symbol strings to

* A vector is a trajectory through various addresses in a state space.

assemble particles from bits instead of using numbers to represent particles. Once things are dead-simple at the most basic level – at the very bottom of the model – the particle component level – perhaps the mathematics of measurement will become more clear."

"Let's see, symbol strings," Sasha thought out loud, "those would just be strings of individual bits. A particle would simply be represented by a specific collection of bits."

"Exactly," Bruce said, "which would have the result, as Stu said, of defining each particle in terms of the smallest unit of information that's possible in information theory: a single yes-or-no bit, one or zero."

"Stu, that's a wonderful suggestion. I'll work on getting the symbol strings into the particle loader," Jim said. "Using the smallest possible unit of information to represent a particle will qualify as a very atomic step and we're atomic guys here."

"I'll look at how our model can potentially be expressed in matrix algebra," Sasha volunteered.

"Say," Bruce said, "has anyone heard from Brownie and Dr. Z about recruiting Thog?"

"Yes, it would be good to hear what Thog thinks," Stu said. "I believe he could help, even though it's a long shot."

"Gosh, I'd forgotten about them," Jim said. "We haven't heard anything for two days now."

"Should we worry?" Sasha asked.

"Let's get our matrix homework done first, and get the symbol strings in the particle loader," Jim said. "And if they still haven't showed up by tomorrow, I guess we'll have to go look for them."

"Yes, science first," said Sasha.

Chapter 21

The What x What

Chief Lion Ring was still debating standards and didn't notice the new tally sticks, but Chief Bear Ford* of the neighboring Delta tribe, who was more adept in the politics of standard-setting, immediately saw the wisdom of embracing them as their popularity soared.

Armed with tally sticks, Thog took up intertribal trade on a grander scale and, to Mrs. Thog's delight, new commodities now arrived at the Thogs' cave. But as the number of commodities grew, so did the complexity of measuring them. There was more stick notching now, and the problem arose of just what each notch actually represented.

One night at dinner, Thog grumbled: "We need some common standards between tribes. The other day I caught a Delta trying to foist a false-bottomed basket on me. All an accurately notched stick is good for in a case like that is knocking some sense into him."

"Now, now, dear," Mrs. Thog replied, "I heard that Chief Bear Ford of the Deltas plans to begin maintaining standards for both of our tribes. Perhaps things will improve."

---

* Chief Bear Ford was named for the bear-crossing at a river near his native village.

"Oh really? I guess I'm not surprised. Old Lion Ring has ours so confused that you can't measure anything with them, but it's a tricky business, this intertribal standard-setting. In fact, I wonder just how much we should trust either one of these chiefs. Bear Ford is a Delta, after all."

"We'll just have to be cautious," Mrs. Thog said. "Perhaps you should take along a few of your own standards on your travels – baskets, stones, and whatnot. That way you could check the other tribes' standards just for 'good measure.'"

Thog began doing this and found it very helpful. But as the number of commodities continued to increase, things became complicated again.

When exchanging berries, it seemed fair to trade a basket of one type for a similar-size basket of another. When exchanging meat, it seemed fair to weigh the quantities traded by using stones. But when the occasion arose to trade berries and beads for tiger skin and fish, Thog had to try to remember how many beads and baskets of berries it should take to fetch a tiger skin and a stone of fish. He took this up with Mrs. Thog.

"What do you think about all these new commodities, dear?"

"I'm very fond of them," she said, "but there are so many of them, trying to keep track of how much of this might fetch how much of that, and how much of that might fetch how much of this is all becoming confusing. There are so many possibilities it's getting a little out of hand."

"I've noticed the same thing myself."

"There's mastodon, tiger, berries, beads, fish," and she continued counting, ticking them off on her fingers. "I believe there must be at least ten commodities involved by now."

"Hmm, perhaps we should develop a model to keep track of them."

"What do you suggest?"

"Well, let's see. First you have to ask 'what'? Then you have to ask 'what else'? And then, of course, you have to ask, 'how much of what might fetch how much of what else'? For example, how many stones of mastodon might fetch how many baskets of berries?"

"That's an awful lot of whats to keep straight."

"Perhaps something like this would serve," he said, scratching a picture in the dirt.

Mrs. Thog looked over Thog's shoulder as he worked. It took him a little while to draw all of it. "Thogette should be drawing these pictures, not me," he complained. But he kept at it.

Thog's Model

"Your pictures are quite nice, dear," Mrs. Thog said. "And what a nice model! Each pair of commodities has its own address, so I can just notch a pair of sticks – one for the amount of each commodity. I can keep each pair of sticks at its address, perhaps tied together with rawhide. Then I'll be able to tell immediately how much of one commodity in the pair might fetch how much of the other."

"Setting it up may take a few sticks," observed Thog, "and keeping it up may take a little notching, but the model should provide a nice way to keep track of commodity pair possibilities and avoid missing any important ones."

"What do you think we should call it, dear?"

Thog reflected for a moment, "Perhaps we should simply call it our *what x what.*"

"Why, what a lovely name, dear. It's really quite descriptive."

The Thogs began using their what x what and Mrs. Thog began notching pairs of sticks, tying them together and carefully storing them at their address.

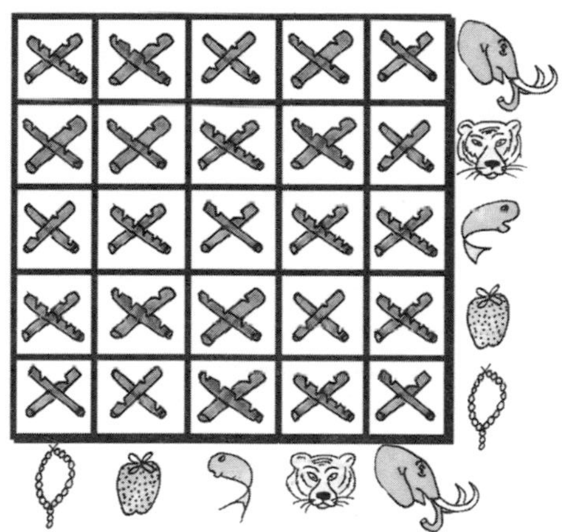

Mrs. Thog's Stick Pairs in Thog's What x What

A practical woman with an eye for efficiency, Mrs. Thog wasn't inclined to do any extraneous stick notching. As she went about her work, she noticed there was one address in the what x what for each commodity where the commodity was paired with itself. Well, she didn't need to notch two sticks to remember that a stone of tiger is a stone of tiger, so she began leaving these addresses in her what x what empty.

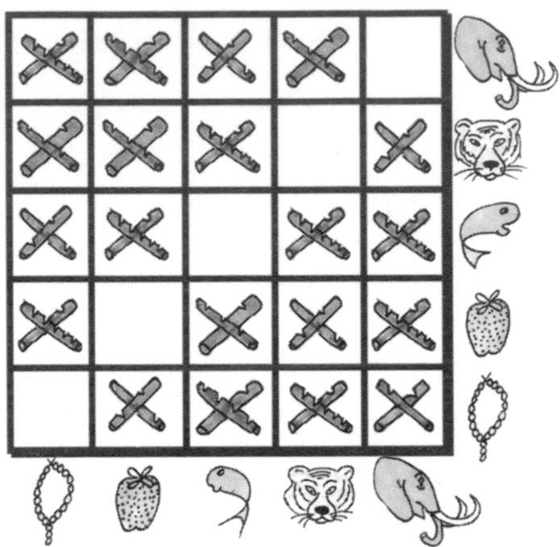

Mrs. Thog Saves a Little Stick Notching

The next thing she noticed is that there were two addresses in the what x what for each commodity pair. For example, there was one for how many stones of tiger might fetch how many stones of fish, and there was another for how many stones of fish might fetch how many stones of tiger. She decided she only needed one of these two addresses in her what x what. Then she would only need to notch one pair of sticks, not two, for a pair like tigers and fish. This efficiency saved space in the cave, which pleased her because she likes to keep a tidy cave.

Mrs. Thog Saves Some Notching and Floor Space

The improved what x what proved a handy record for the Thogs. They could remind themselves of what might fetch what simply by checking a pair of notched sticks at its address in their what x what. Of course, when it came time for the next trade, things might not fetch exactly the amounts her what x what suggested. But when the amounts changed in the next trade, Mrs. Thog just updated her what x what to reflect the newest information.

Chapter 22

Emergent Money

As Mrs. Thog's sources had predicted, Chief Bear Ford took up standard-setting duties for both tribes with zeal. Having quickly embraced tally sticks, he knew a potential new standard when he saw one. He immediately assumed responsibility for all the whats in the what x what and set the elders to work establishing official whats.

Meanwhile the what x what was proving to be so useful for keeping track of commodity relationships that everyone began using it. Trade flourished.

As the Thogs' prosperity increased, so did the number and variety of commodities they enjoyed, and pretty soon this became a problem again.

"Our what x what is getting so big, there's no longer room for it on the cave floor," Mrs. Thog complained. "The number of commodities has doubled. We are up to twenty now, and let's see ... yes, there are one hundred ninety pairs of sticks – three hundred eighty sticks in total!* No doubt we'll soon have even more. I do like all these new commodities, but our what x what has become unmanageable."

---

*If you want to check Mrs. Thog's counting, you can use the equation: N [(N-1)/2] where N is the number of possible commodities. To compute the number of sticks required, you then multiply the number of addresses by two because each address has two sticks.

Thog considered it a serious problem when Mrs. Thog complained, as she rarely did. "Hmm," he said, studying the what x what, "perhaps, you could save some floor space if we chose one commodity as a standard by which to measure all the other commodity relationships. Then as new commodities are added, our what x what would only get bigger in one direction instead of two. Plus it would only take one stick instead of two for each commodity."

"Which commodity would you suggest?" she asked.

Thog, knowing she was partial to them, said, "We could use your beads."

"Oh yes," Mrs. Thog beamed, "of course."

"They're not only lovely, they're the easiest of our commodities to carry around."

Mrs. Thog, who wears them around every day, replied, "That's true."

When the Thogs began using beads to measure other commodities, they saved a lot of stick notching as well as a lot of floor space. Now their twenty-commodity what x what required only nineteen sticks.

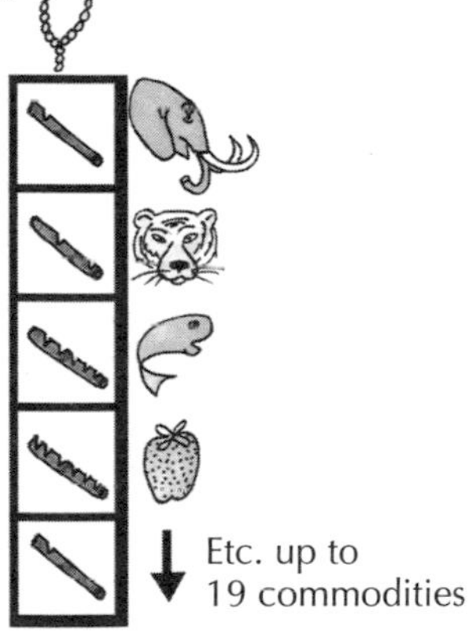

The Thogs' What x What Using Beads As a Standard

The Thogs began using beads just in the nick of time, because the number of commodities in their world began to grow rapidly and the complexity of a what x what grows much more rapidly than the number of commodities involved. (For example, a what x what for two thousand commodities, absent beads as a standard for measure, would have about two million commodity-pair addresses and require nearly four million sticks. Imagine the mess this would have made on Mrs. Thog's floor!)

Thog was influential in trading circles and others soon picked up on the efficiency of using beads for measuring the other commodities in their what x whats. And, as more and more traders carried beads around on their trading junkets to use in measuring other commodities, they soon began trading the beads themselves for these other commodities. When they did this, they were using beads as both a standard of measure <u>and</u> a medium of exchange.

"Dear, your beads are a triumphant success," Thog said one night at dinner. "Now that we're both measuring other commodities with them and exchanging them for other commodities, we're killing two birds with one stone."

"How lovely, dear. What do you suppose we should call such a commodity?"

"Hmm," Thog said, "something serious, I guess. Perhaps we should call it *money*."

"Why, I should think people will take money quite seriously."

With money invented and their what x what back under control, the Thogs' dinner conversation turned to Thog's upcoming trading trip. Showing Mrs. Thog his map, Thog explained his plans to visit thirteen other tribes.

"The routes on your map remind me of the what x what," she said. (Mrs. Thog was still thinking about how fast the what x what addresses had grown with each new commodity before they invented money.)

"Really?" Thog asked, looking up from his map in surprise. "How is that?"

"Well," she said, "it's difficult to determine the shortest route for your trip because the number of routes appears to grow very rapidly each time a new address is added. Even though there aren't very many addresses, there appear to be a huge number of possible routes between them. To determine the shortest route you would have to consider them all."

"I've never tried to determine the shortest route," Thog said. "Usually I just pick what looks like a pretty good one and then take things a step at a time. If I have to double back or make a detour, the beads are so easy to carry that I don't mind."

"Very well, dear. I just noticed the *route complexity* and thought I'd mention it. I'm glad the beads are making things easier for you."

"That's a nice name for it – route complexity," Thog said.

(Mrs. Thog was right. When Jim heard the story later, he calculated the number of routes and it turns out there were 3,113,510,400 possible routes for Thog's travel between only thirteen destinations!* This is also known as The Trav-

---

*This is computed (13x12x11.....x2x1)/2. You divide by two because you can take each route in either of two directions.

eling Salesman Problem, which is a popular example of computational limitations. When a large number of destinations are involved, computing the shortest itinerary still remains beyond the capability of today's most powerful computers, even with Jim doing the coding.)

Chapter 23

Transaction Bites

With beads in hand, Chief Lion Ring's elders had less to argue about, so they spent less time in his cave debating standards and more time outside spending money. Chief Lion Ring, brave though he'd been in confrontations with lions or rival tribesmen, just couldn't adjust to the new times. He retired to his cave full of antiquated standards memorabilia and was soon forgotten.

Chief Bear Ford, however, was quick to add money to the list of standards he maintained for both tribes, and due to its widespread popularity, Bear Ford thrived.

Thog also found money increasingly useful. Whenever he returned from a trading trip, he would count the beads in his pouch to see how well he'd done, and then he counted all the beads in the family pouch as a measure of their general level of prosperity.

But even though money simplified the Thogs' what x what record of what various things might fetch in trade, and provided a nice summary of the results of their actual trading, they still needed to keep track of each transaction – the commodities they traded and how much each cost or fetched – in terms of money. So as the number of commodities grew, the cave once again grew cluttered with the notched sticks from various transactions. The Thogs called this problem *stick complexity*.

For example, when Mrs. Thog traded berries for beads she not only notched a stick as "ten beads' worth of berries" – a money record – she notched another stick as "one basket worth of berries" – a commodity record. Sometimes Thog helped Mrs. Thog notch the sticks, but he was easily bored and tended to abandon notching duty to go tiger hunting whenever possible.

From one such hunt, which lasted about a week, he returned with a nice but smallish tiger. He had tracked a huge and ferocious one for two days, but it got away. (In fact, if you want to know the truth, it was actually the other way around; it was Thog, not the tiger, who got away.)

While Thog was hunting tigers, Mrs. Thog had a lot of time to consider the frustrations of stick complexity. Consequently she was on a slightly different page from Thog on his first night home.

"How was your hunt, dear?" Mrs. Thog asked.

"So-so. The best one got away."

"Well, you did bring home a very nice one."

"Thanks, but the one that got away was a real beauty."

"While you were away I've been thinking about stick complexity."

"Yes?" Thog said, his mind still on the one that got away. He'd known the moment he saw its tracks that it was a big one, a beauty...

"Have you noticed that a trade often consists of getting to yes or no about a number of individual components?"

Mrs. Thog asked. "For example, it might involve exchanging thirty beads for three beads' worth of berries, twenty beads' worth of tiger meat, and seven beads' worth of skins. Each of these yes-or-no components requires a separate pair of sticks. I do believe it is all these components that are causing stick complexity to get out of hand."

"Why, I suppose so," he replied, picturing his final moments with the tiger: He'd thought he was tracking the tiger, but as he peered intently at where the tracks led, he heard an ominous growl behind him. The tiger was tracking him…

"Do you think we should have a name for the general notion of these yes-or-no component pairs?"

"Huh?" Thog said. "I'm sorry, dear, what did you just ask me?" Spinning around to get his spear in position, he was about to take the tiger, when he slipped and only escaped by dropping his spear and scrambling up a handy tree. And just in the nick of time. The tiger was snarling and biting at his heels as adrenaline pumped through him…

"I asked if you thought we should have a name for the components of a trade. The components that are causing all this stick complexity," Mrs. Thog said, by now a little exasperated.

"I suppose we should," he said, trying now to find his way down from the tree with the snarling tiger beneath it and back into his conversation with Mrs. Thog.

"Well then, what do you suppose the name should be?" she said, trying to remain patient.

"Name. Yes. Let's see. How about, let's see, hmm … ahh … how about *bite*?" he asked, still thinking of the bite he'd barely escaped.

"Bite?" Mrs. Thog asked, puzzled. "What a curious name! But if you like it, I suppose it will do. At least it's short and easy to remember."

Naming bites that night didn't altogether solve the problem of stick complexity, but the Thogs got a good start on the problem by identifying the important yes or nos involved in a transaction and figuring out a name for them. At least now they were on the same page as they went on to tackle the problem of stick complexity bite by bite.

I asked Thog, "How did you ever get your spear back?"

"I waited until the tiger left. Then I waited a little longer just to be sure. And eventually I climbed down the tree slowly and very carefully," he said.

"A step at a time?"

"Exactly," Thog said.

"Just like we're heading towards the true meaning of debits and credits?" Dr. Z. asked.

"Yes, bite by bite, dear," Mrs. Thog replied.

Chapter 24

The Who x When

Beads gained ever-wider acceptance as money, and commerce flourished. But stick complexity kept growing and Mrs. Thog had just about reached the limit of her patience. One night she said to Thog, "There simply must be a better way to organize all these sticks. There are so many, I get them confused, and they're underfoot all the time. The cave is a complete mess."

"Why, yes," Thog said, "I'm sure there must be a better way."

"At least the sticks for keeping track of transactions are nicely organized in bites now, but there are an awful lot of bites in all these transactions, and each bite still takes two sticks. Maybe we could do something clever with the bites and get the cave a little better organized."

"Yes, dear," he said. "We probably need another model. Let's see. What are the important yes or nos about the bites in each transaction?"

"Well, one is whether someone is getting or giving something."

"Yes, and another is who is doing the getting and giving."

"Of course."

"And then there's <u>when</u> the giving and getting is supposed to happen."

"Yes," she said. "Do you remember the first time that 'when' came up, in our first dealings with the Deltas?"

"Of course, just like yesterday. That's when you suggested sticks in the first place, so we could start a transaction without having to finish it right away – a terrific idea!"

"Thank you, although I must say, the sticks have gotten out of hand."

"That can happen with the best of ideas," he consoled. "But can you think of any other important yes or nos that occur in each transaction?"

"Well, no," she said. "I can't."

"OK," he said. "So now all we have to do is figure out how to put these in a model."

They decided to use adding for getting and subtracting for giving. Adding and subtracting seemed to work pretty well, and the Thogs had been doing these things for nearly as long as they'd been counting.

"Of course, we could only add and subtract the notches on some of the sticks," Mrs. Thog said.

"True," Thog said. "It would work nicely for notches on all the bead sticks, but adding or subtracting notches on a stick that represents baskets and a stick that represents stones would be less useful."

"But still," Mrs. Thog said, "just getting the bites organized would be a substantial improvement, even if it only made sense to add and subtract <u>some</u> of the sticks."

"Well," he said, remembering the what x what, "with

getting and giving handled, we're left with whos and whens, a *who x when model*. Let's see, the yes-or-no possibilities for the whos are either mine or yours ..."

Mrs. Thog looked puzzled.

"In the general case, I meant to say," he hastily corrected himself. "In the family case, of course, it would be ours or theirs."

"I should think so!" Mrs. Thog retorted.

"And I suppose at the time of a trade," he continued, still trying to recover from his faux pas over the whos, "a when must be either now or later."

"Yes," she said, "those would seem to be the yes-or-no possibilities for the whens."

"Do you suppose something like this would serve?" he asked, scratching a picture in the dirt.

	Now	Later
Mine	Mine Now	Mine Later
Yours	Yours Now	Yours Later

Thog's Model for Organizing Bites

Thog's picture looked like a what x what. It showed a box with four addresses: *mine-now, yours-now, mine-later,* and *yours-later.* "These," he pointed out to Mrs. Thog, "would appear to represent all the possible yes-or-no answers to questions of yours or mine and now or later for every possible transaction."

"What a lovely model for organizing the transaction bites!" Mrs. Thog exclaimed. "Since it represents all the possibilities for any transaction, I shouldn't think our who x when will ever need to get any bigger. That is a nice advantage over our old what x what, where the number of addresses tended to get out of hand before money."

With Thog's who x when in hand, Mrs. Thog was finally able to organize all of her bite sticks. The Thogs shared their idea with others, and pretty soon traders everywhere were organizing their sticks using the who x when. It not only served the hunter-gatherers, it eventually went on to serve the Agrarian Age, the Dark Ages, the Renaissance, the Industrial Revolution, and the Internet economy, as well as the transition economies between them.

By simply adding up the money in the four basic addresses of the who x when and expressing each address as a single number, the Thogs were on their way to preparing what we now call "financial statements."

"Oh yes, oh yes," Dr. Z blurted. "Of course! It's the conceptual framework for financial statements – all financial statements, everywhere! Oh my!"

You might think she was overreacting, but she did go on to explain what she was so excited about. Whipping a sharpened pencil out of her backpack, she drew a picture.

	Income Statement Now	Balance Sheet Later
Mine	Revenues	Assets
Yours	Expenses	Liabilities

Dr. Z's Version of Thog's Model

Then she explained that the two now-addresses of the who x when – "revenues" and "expenses" – summarize components of transactions that have occurred up until now. You just subtract one from the other to get "income" or "loss," which is the equation for the "income statement." The two later-addresses – "assets" and "liabilities" – summarize the components of transactions that remain to be completed later. You just subtract one of these from the other to get what we call "equity." This is the equation for the "balance sheet."

"It's the accounting equation in a box," Dr. Z said with delight.

"Yes, dear," said Mrs. Thog, "but back then we called them *recipes* rather than equations – the recipes of commerce – like mastodon plus herbs equals rack of mastodon."

"Oh yes, like with the Deltas," Dr. Z said. "I'm sorry, I didn't mean to get ahead of the story."

"Why don't we just skip on ahead?" Junior suggested, still hoping to avoid certain parts of the story that involved him.

"Oh no," Dr. Z said. "I want to hear the whole thing – every episode"

Chapter 25

Rendezvous at the Cave

After Dr. Z's excitement over the who x when had subsided, we decided to take a break from the Thogs' story and just enjoy a social evening in the cave. I'll admit, the story had carried me along. I'd completely lost track of time and hadn't had a second thought about Wall Street since my first night in the cave. And now, at our little party, I was finally going to hear the story of Thog's mastodon hunt with Ray Kurzweil.

Junior had whetted my curiosity about mastodon hunting on our first day with the Thogs, and I was doubly curious about this particular hunt. I've known Ray for years and admired his many scientific accomplishments, but I'd never thought of him as a mastodon hunter. So I could hardly wait to hear what happened.

Let me tell you, Thog's reputation as a storyteller is richly deserved. He described so vividly how he and Ray had assembled their spears, of just the right heft and size, that I felt as if I were right there beside him in the woods, tracking the huge beasts. He painted a rich picture, and the suspense built during the final stalk. I was holding my breath just as he began moving in for the kill.

And then he stopped abruptly in midsentence. After a long silence, he said, "I thought I heard something."

We were all as quiet as possible, and I wondered if this was a storytelling technique. But then Thog got up from the dinner table and went to the door, opened it ever so quietly and listened intently, staring into the dark. Then we heard it, too.

"Yoodeelaadeehoo" came echoing faintly up the mountain, as if by some virtual-reality programming error we had been transported from Thog's mastodon hunt to a Swiss ski outing in a Warren Miller movie.

"Yoodeelaadeehoo," Thog answered at full volume, the sound reverberating around the cave and rattling the dinner dishes.

"Why, I do believe it's Stu Kauffman come to visit," he declared.

Sure enough, it was – and not just Stu, unmistakable in his purple parka. Jim, Bruce, and Sasha were trudging up the mountain with him, chatting away amiably like scientists seem to do.

Well, it was quite a scene in the cave. Thog gave Stu a big hug, introduced everyone to everyone, and put more chairs around the table. Junior and Thogette set more places, Mrs. Thog brought out more food, and we all sat down. We had a lot to talk about, but the hikers were hungry, so there wasn't much conversation while they ate dinner. Then the catching-up began.

Stu said, "We were beginning to worry about Brownie and Dr. Z. They've been gone for two days now, so we came looking for them."

Mrs. Thog apologized. "Oh my, I believe we lost track of time. You see, we became involved in the story of debits and credits, beginning with what Dr. Z says you call quantum decoherence."

"Really?" Bruce said. "Beginning with quantum decoherence? You guys have been doing some physics up here, I guess."

"Sort of," Dr. Z said.

"Well, Dr. Z, have you found the Thogs' story helpful?" Stu said.

"Oh yes! But we've just begun. We haven't even come to debits and credits yet."

"Say Stu," Thog asked, "how are things in Santa Fe on the quantum economics front?"

"Not good, I'm afraid. We were hoping you were coming to Santa Fe to help us with it."

"Oh, we are!" Mrs. Thog exclaimed, anxious lest Thog miss the opportunity to do something useful. "Thog mentioned your lovely invitation. It's just that there's been so much going on."

"Are you still having a problem with the economic particle collider?" Dr. Z asked. "Didn't the carbon rods absorb the excess energy?"

"Nope. I'm afraid we were on the wrong track there," Bruce said.

"Carbon rods?" Junior asked. "What's an economic particle collider?"

"Oh, it's a model," Jim said.

"Cool," said Junior. "Nice name, too – collider."

Thogette smiled at Bruce and added, "We love models!"

He replied, "So do we!"

"Perhaps it's just a matter of inventing something to solve your problem?" Junior said with the confidence of an experienced teenage inventor.

"Yes, that's exactly what we need to do," Sasha said. "We need to invent a pair-wise measurement construct for interacting agents to use when exchanging economic particles that results in an emergent binary measure on a rugged biological fitness landscape."

"I'm afraid I'm not sure what you're talking about," Junior said, looking perplexed.

With an eye on Bruce, Thogette said to Junior, "Oh, we'll work all that out. It's just terminology. We like inventing things just as much as we like modeling. It'll be fun."

"Who knows?" Thog said. "Perhaps your solution has already been invented by someone else. Stu tells me this sometimes happens in science."

"Well," Bruce replied, "we've certainly checked every possible scientific journal on this subject and come up with nothing."

Thogette gave Bruce another winning smile and said, "We'll just have to have fun inventing something then."

I wasn't sure Bruce caught her undertone, but Mrs. Thog did.

Finally Mrs. Thog said, "It's getting late and things are getting a little complicated here. Let's take a step at a time. First, all of you must stay overnight. It's too late and too dark for hiking back down the mountain, and we have lots of guest rooms. In the morning we'll begin with a nice breakfast. Then we'll get everyone on the same page. And after that we'll figure out if we Thogs can somehow help with Dr. Z's debits and credits as well as whatever you need invented for your quantum economics."

Well, there's no arguing with Mrs. Thog, so we all went off to our separate rooms for the night.

Chapter 26

Getting on the Same Page

Getting everyone on the same page took a little while. It started before breakfast, continued through the meal, and went on into the morning.

"Dr. Z," Bruce said, "I didn't think of you as a physicist when you left Santa Fe, but after your description of decoherence I'm having to change my mind."

"Thank you, Bruce. I would think standards of measure are just as important in science as they are in accounting."

"Absolutely," Bruce said. "Measurement is everything in science."

"We were looking for a binary record based on ordered pairs, and your stick pairs and bites comprise just such a record," Sasha said.

"Yep, and we didn't have to invent it after all," Bruce said. "It turns out the Thogs had already done it for us."

"Your bites are much like computing bytes," Jim added, "except they come in various sizes – one bite might consist of more or fewer yes-or-no bits than another – whereas computing bytes always contain exactly eight bits. There's probably an etymological connection."

"This diet chart can't be right. I know I'm taking smaller bites than it shows here and I haven't lost a single pound."

"Yes," Mrs. Thog said, thinking of Thog's table manners, "sometimes bites do occur in various sizes."

"Well," Junior offered, "it appears that what you guys call Tit for Tat is the same thing as our win-win strategy."

"Yes," Sasha said, "which scientists have confirmed to be evolutionarily robust in countless experiments and which is why we are using it in the collider."

"Not surprisingly, countless experiments and a few thousand years of experience have a great deal in common," Stu said.

"We were looking for important something x somethings, and you had already discovered two of them: the what x what and the who x when," Sasha said. "As your commerce developed, the dimensions of your what x what grew larger with each new commodity you experienced and your who x when recorded all of this diversity, but never grew larger, because it contained your transactions within the basic binaries that are common to all transactions."

"You know, Dr. Z, it sure would have made things easier for us scientists if you had suggested using matrices in the collider," Jim said. "Even if you had suggested using equations in a box, we might have had a clue you were talking about something mathematical. But 'debits and credits' – those words could mean anything."

Junior grinned at Dr. Z.

"Well, there's no question about it now," Bruce said. "Agents in the collider have gotta have what x whats and who x whens. They are just the record formats we've been looking for."

"I'm sorry about the terminology," Dr. Z said. "Actually, I now like the terms 'what x what' and 'who x when' even better than 'matrices.' They're more to the recordkeeping point. From here on out, I'm going to stop saying 'the books' and use the new-old terms instead!"

"How about 'debits' and 'credits'?" Jim asked. "Are you ready to stop using them as well?"

"Maybe a little later, but not quite yet. First I'd like to know their true meaning."

Junior grinned at Dr. Z again.

"Does your model require a lot of computing?" Thog asked, to change the subject so Junior would quit grinning at Dr. Z.

"Quite a bit," Jim said. "But so far it's still manageable. Why do you ask?"

"Oh," Stu said, "I bet Thog's thinking about Mrs. Thog's route complexity problem – what we call the Traveling Salesman Problem, the problem of the uncomputability of all the routes between addresses in a model with a lot of addresses."

"I suppose you don't have to compute all the routes possible in your collider," Thog said, "just those the agents have actually used so far. Sort of a step-at-a-time kind of thing."

"Exactly. And that's why we need to model these things from the bottom up," Jim said. "Coming at all the possibilities from the top down is simply not computable. It's a non-starter."

"I like the idea of an agent who acts on his own behalf from the bottom up," Thogette said, eyeing Bruce.

Sasha, who was not on quite the same page as Thogette, said, "Well, we have a lot more work to do on the collider model. Maybe when we make all these changes to the collider, we'll finally get producers, consumers, and money."

"All this may lead to various possibilities," Mrs. Thog said, looking at Bruce and Thogette and smiling.

"Then we'd better hear another episode," said Stu. (Stu loves a good story almost as much as a hunter-gatherer.)

"Let's see," Thog said, "where were we?"

"Well, I believe Junior was just about to invent agriculture," Mrs. Thog said.

"Junior invented agriculture?" Sasha said, incredulous.

Junior blushed.

"Oh yeah," Thogette said. "It doesn't have much to do with your model, but he did invent it."

"Well, let's hear about it anyway," Dr. Z enthused.

Chapter 27

The Invention of Agriculture

Chief Bear Ford recognized the who x when as an important standard and took responsibility for maintaining it. People began using it to tidy up their bite sticks, and the grumbling about stick complexity died down.

With the cave better organized, Mrs. Thog turned her attention to her gathering chores and one day she noticed that some of the things she gathered appeared to grow from seeds. She collected some of these and planted them herself in some plots she called her *garden*. But before you know it, a problem developed. The plants attracted wild sheep, which began hanging around nibbling the tender shoots.

Mrs. Thog had recipes for sheep, which were tasty enough, but the family preferred mastodon and tiger. Junior wasn't allowed to hunt mastodon or tigers yet, but his mother decided sheep were a different matter. So sometimes she sent Junior out to bring one in for dinner, and other times she sent him out to shoo them away.

Junior liked getting a sheep for dinner. They were exactly the right size for his small spear and good practice for tiger hunting with his dad – his main dream! But Junior found shooing a bother, and he was doing a lot more shooing than spearing. There must be more efficient ways to deal with the garden-eating sheep, he thought.

"Hey, Mom," he said, one afternoon, "I think we should separate some of the addresses in your garden by planting two gardens and building something to enclose each of them. This would keep the sheep out of the first garden so we can plant your favorite things there, and we could plant some things the sheep like in the second garden and keep the sheep in there with something. We might call that something a *fence*. Then I wouldn't have to shoo them or chase them as far when you want to cook one for dinner."

"Why, Junior, what a wonderful idea!" Mrs. Thog exclaimed. "You must tell the family about it."

The family agreed it was a good idea, and Thog decided to call Junior's garden-and-fence combination *agriculture*.

So that's how Junior invented agriculture – with a little help from his mom, of course. But the family conversation didn't stop there.

"Dear," Thog said, "now that Junior has invented agriculture, don't you think he is mature enough to go on a tiger hunt with me?"

At this, Junior got so excited he could barely contain himself. While the Thogs almost never disagree in front of the children, this subject proved to be an exception. Mrs. Thog put her foot down: no way, not old enough. Thog and Junior were disappointed, of course, but Thogette, jealous that Junior was getting so much attention simply for inventing agriculture, enjoyed her mother's response a lot.

Maybe it didn't get him a tiger-hunt, but Junior's invention caught on rapidly. Agriculture migrated from the Thogs' old neighborhood in the Fertile Crescent, extending from Jericho north to Damascus and Syria, then southeast down the Tigris and Euphrates River valleys through Babylon to Uruk and Ur. And then it caught on around the world.

Thanks to fences enclosing Mrs. Thog's berry plot, there were plenty of berries and Thog could have his favorite dessert almost every night. Now that they had a sheepfold, Mrs. Thog began spinning wool, which added variety to their wardrobes. And they found that if they sold their sheep "on the hoof," they fetched more beads than dead ones did, since they stayed fresh longer. So, thanks to agriculture, they had more, different, and better-quality commodities.

As the Thogs' story of agriculture came to a close, Thogette, who had chosen a seat next to Bruce, whispered to him: "Actually, the family member whose invention is relevant to your particle collider is Uncle Pi Thogarus. He invented geometry while mapping Junior's agricultural plots."

"Really?" Bruce said.

"Thogette's flirting!" Junior taunted.

"Children!" Mrs. Thog said, smiling and doing her best to sound stern.

Chapter 28

Thogette's Tokens

Mrs. Thog was spending a lot of time on sticks. Too much, in fact. They were driving her nuts. As had happened before, there were too many sticks and too many of them looked alike. Of course, she could move all her sticks to a larger cave like the Bear Fords had, but this would involve moving her garden and Junior's fences – a lot of work. Mrs. Thog was looking for a better way.

One day as she and Thogette cleaned up around the fire pit after a meal, Thogette spilled the washing-up water in the dirt. (Thogette doesn't like washing up, so sometimes she's a little careless.)

"Well, dear," said her mother, who hadn't noticed the spill, "it looks as if we're finished here. If you'll start the garden work, I'll come help you as soon as I tidy up the cave. For the life of me, I have to figure out a better way to handle all these sticks. They all look the same and it's practically impossible to tell one from another."

"Hey, Mom," Thogette said. "Have you noticed this dirt? If it gets wet and hot at the same time, it gets really hard. Come take a look." (Thogette, as it turns out, had just discovered clay.)

"Hmm … I do believe you're right. How very interesting! I never noticed this before."

"You know, Mom, I'll bet we could make some little models of your various commodities from this wet dirt and then bake them until they get hard. Models would be easier to tell apart than sticks, and they'd be fun to make as well."

(A lot more fun than working in the garden, Thogette thought.)

That afternoon Thogette and Mrs. Thog made some clay models to show Thog and Junior at dinnertime. Thogette has artistic talent, so they turned out nicely.

Thog and Junior were duly impressed with the models and Thogette's idea of using them to replace sticks, so the whole family agreed to adopt them. Knowing Thog's weak spot for naming things, Thogette asked, "What do you think they should be called, Daddy – the little models, I mean?"

She would have preferred a name with more flair, but Thog suggested *tokens*. Then the conversation turned to various other ways tokens might be used to improve things.

"Can't you take them with you trading, Daddy?" she asked. "You know, instead of all your sticks?"

"Well," Thog replied, "the real problem, whether you are using sticks or tokens, is keeping track of which pair represents which bite. Tokens for one bite might get mixed up with those for another, just as sticks do."

But Thogette, looking for a further excuse to make models instead of gardening, wasn't about to take no for an answer.

"I see. Well, say there are ten beads and two stones of fish involved in a bite. Couldn't we just bake up ten tokens that look like beads and two that look like fish, and then bake these into a hollow clay ball representing the bite? You could carry these balls around without getting the tokens mixed up, Daddy. In fact, you could send a ball like this to another trader along with the goods without even going along yourself, and then when the goods arrived, someone you trust could break it open and check the tokens against the commodities. This would help Mom keep the bites straight, reduce route complexity, and save you time."

"It does sound better, but someone would have to bake the clay balls and tokens."

"Of course! I plan to do that myself."

What could Thog do but agree? Thogette had him wrapped around her little finger anyway.

Junior was jealous of Thogette's new role and hoped his mom would not allow it. After all, she seemed to have an attitude about her children experiencing new things – tiger hunting, for example.

But Mrs. Thog quickly dashed this hope. "What a wonderful idea, Thogette!"

Hmm, thought Junior, it looks like Mom's in a receptive mood. He seized the opportunity: "While we're having new experiences here, how about my tiger hunt, Mom?"

Mrs. Thog, swept up in the moment, and to Junior's complete surprise, said, "Oh, why not?"

So it was a win-win evening for both Thogette and Junior.

The next morning Thogette began baking balls and tokens, and in no time they caught on. They were soon in use throughout the Chaldean-Babylonian, Assyrian, and Sumerian civilizations. In fact, in 7000 BC, the neighboring Sumerians, quick to pick up on a good idea, named the new clay balls "bullae." It disappointed Thog that he had neglected to name them himself – after all, a bulla was only a bitc filled with tokens – but he was proud of Thogette for inventing them.

Chapter 29

Writing and Arithmetic

Much as Thogette had envisioned, tokens and bullae proved efficient for Thog in his trading travels. And Mrs. Thog appreciated the fact that tokens were easier to tell apart than sticks, because they had different shapes, which reduced the confusion in her what x what and who x when recordkeeping.

But there was a serious problem with tokens. You could put multiple notches on one stick to represent multiple units of one commodity (20 notches for 20 sheep), but it took one token for each unit of the commodity when you represented it with tokens. If you wanted to exchange one sheep for 20 beads, you needed a bulla with one sheep token and 20 bead tokens. So, there were soon even more tokens than there had been sticks, and token complexity became a faster-growing problem than stick complexity had ever been.

"You know," Thog said, "sometimes I miss the old sticks. There was a certain satisfaction in a well-notched stick, if you know what I mean."

"Why, yes, dear," Mrs. Thog said. "Sometimes you no sooner get rid of one kind of complexity than another rears its head."

Meanwhile, Thogette found herself baking more and more tokens to fill all the bullae. At first it had been fun – it certainly beat digging in the garden – but pretty soon she grew bored. So, to pass the time while the tokens and bullae were in the oven, she began doodling on the outside of some of the unbaked bullae, drawing little pictures of the tokens that were contained inside. One day Mrs. Thog caught her doodling.

"Why, Thogette, what are you doing there?"

Thogette, fearing that to admit she was bored would send her back to the garden, thought quickly on her feet. "I'm inscribing these bullae so you won't need to break them open to count the tokens. You'll know how many tokens are in a bulla just by counting the symbols on the outside of it. Come to think of it, you won't even need the tokens!"

"What a magnificent idea!" Mrs. Thog. exclaimed. "You must tell your father."

That night Thogette explained her new idea for inscribing bullae with pictures representing the tokens they contained. "What should we name this idea Daddy?" she asked.

And Thog, after some deliberation, said, "I suggest we call it *writing*."

Thog took written bullae on his trading junkets, and in almost no time at all, Thogette's practice of writing caught on throughout the Fertile Crescent. Writing was very efficient and this simplification permitted more trading and increased prosperity.

But increased prosperity brought an onslaught of commodities, and all the writing grew tedious. When a large number of sheep were involved in a transaction – 315, for example – it was tiring to write the same symbol 315 times, and sometimes Mrs. Thog developed writer's cramp.

Meanwhile Thogette continued baking her clay and improving her written descriptions of the tokens. After she developed her routine, she had plenty of time to think, and one day she had a truly magnificent idea. Writing had been a pretty good idea, rivaling Junior's invention of agriculture, but this one, she knew, was even better. So she spent the afternoon planning how to present it to the family with the most dramatic effect.

Junior and Thog were somewhat distracted at dinner that night. They'd been busy planning, too: they had tigers to hunt. But Thogette knew how to get her father's attention. "Daddy, you know the Sumerians were pretty quick to name bullae, even though I invented them, but I so wish you had named them instead."

Thog turned from Junior to Thogette.

"But it doesn't matter anymore," she said. "Bullae are obsolete now, even the written ones."

"Obsolete? Already?"

"Yes, Daddy. As long as I'm writing symbols anyway, I plan not only to create a symbol for each commodity token — what you might think of as its description — but also a symbol for the <u>number</u> of each commodity. Then I won't have to draw the same symbol over and over, which is boring and causes writer's cramp. With number symbols, we won't need the round bullae anymore. We can just use flat tablets of clay, and for each bite we can simply write <u>both</u> the description <u>and</u> the corresponding number for it on the tablet. And then, of course, we can add and subtract the numbers and whatnot just as we've been doing for some time."

Warming to her case, Thogette continued, "Being able to write them down will make it easier to keep track when the adding and subtracting beome complex. The flat tablets will require less clay and baking than bullae and be easier to carry. Both traders in a transaction can see everything they need to know right on the tablet. In short, numbers and tablets will be cheaper, better, easier to use, and more flexible!"

By now Thogette had the entire family's attention. Even Junior was impressed. They sat in stunned silence contemplating Thogette's magnificent idea.

When everyone had absorbed its full import, Thogette purred: "So what would you like to name my new idea, Daddy?"

After he had composed himself and given it his best thought, Thog said, "Well, with the adding and subtracting of numbers and so forth, I suggest we name Thogette's invention *arithmetic*."

So this is how Thogette invented both writing and arithmetic, which goes to show there is no limit to what the teenage mind can accomplish when the alternative is to perform a boring chore.

Dr. Z was ecstatic. "To think all this was discovered by a teenager – a young girl! What a triumph for us girls!"

Bruce beamed at Thogette.

Thogette blushed.

Chapter 30

Mrs. Thog's Pers

The next morning the Thogs resumed the story with an update on Chief Bear Ford, who had good political instincts and didn't take credit for writing and arithmetic. Instead he announced that by protecting money and who x whens, he'd created an environment that fostered innovation. He cited writing and arithmetic as examples.

As to the money, Chief Bear Ford had a big idea. He began putting his own picture on the metal coins that were beginning to replace beads as money, so everyone would know what he looked like. This ended up working well for Chief Bear Ford and has been popular with chiefs ever since.

Meanwhile, Mrs. Thog was considering how best to use Thogette's new ideas of writing and arithmetic to simplify her recordkeeping complexity problems.

She began by organizing her new tablets in the who x when and what x what formats. After all, it was sticks, tokens, and bullae that had been causing all the complexity; there was nothing wrong with the basic models.

She finished with the what x what on the first morning. She simply wrote the symbol for each commodity on a freshly baked clay tablet and, after it, the monetary number representing what one unit of that commodity might fetch.

Hmm ..., this was easier than I expected, she thought to herself. It only took a couple of tablets. (Mrs. Thog writes fairly small in a neat, tidy hand.) I may as well get started on the who x when.

To write the bites in her who x when, Mrs. Thog needed a symbol to indicate whether a bite involved giving or getting. She had been using adding for getting, and subtracting for giving, and she decided to use a "+" for bites she was adding and call it a *plus*, and to use a "-" for those she was subtracting and call it a *minus*.

Once she began marking the bites with these symbols, the process began to take a little longer. For one thing, there were a lot of bites. And for another, each bite required two number symbols, one for money and one for the commodity that belonged with it.

To keep track of which was which, she decided to write the money number for each bite above its commodity measure. For example, she wrote "$^{4}_{1}$" representing four beads that belong together with one basket of berries.

For the balance of the afternoon, Mrs. Thog continued working her way through the who x when, bite by bite. "Let's see, twelve beads belong together with two stones of sheep," she muttered. "Nine beads belong together with three tiger skins, this belongs together with that, that belongs together with this … belongs together with, belongs together, belongs …" After several hours she had muttered "belongs together with" so many times, she was practically numb. Besides it's a real tongue-twister to say it fast many times in a row. (Try it.)

By dinnertime Mrs. Thog still hadn't finished converting the who x when to arithmetic, so she decided to discuss the belongs-together-with problem with the family. It took a while to get around to the topic, since Thog and Junior were deep into tiger-hunt talk.

"Not to interrupt, but there is something I would like to ask about before it gets too late."

"Yes, of course, dear," Thog said, "What is it?"

"I'm having trouble converting the who x when to arithmetic."

She explained the "+" and "-" symbols she was using for each bite, the names she had chosen for them, and her using two number symbols to represent each bite. Everyone agreed that she was going about the conversion in a good way and they liked the symbols and the names "plus" and "minus."

"But I'm stuck on the matter of a short name," she said.

"Oh?" Thog said, brightening.

"And," she added hastily, "on the matter of a symbol."

"A symbol as well?" Thogette asked, her interest piqued.

"Yes, both."

Thog, who knows Mrs. Thog's habit of talking to herself when she's working, came up with a short, easy-to-mutter name. "How about just saying *per*? For example, four beads per basket?"

"Why, what a lovely short name. It should save me a great deal of time."

"And you could use a little diagonal line for a per," Thogette said, inscribing it "/" on a handy clay tablet. "It's like using one stick to symbolize the two sticks in the pair that have been replaced by numbers."

"Yes, that should be quite easy to write," Mrs. Thog said, "as well as a reminder of how many sticks we're saving by using all these symbols."

"Let's see," Thog said. "Getting to yes or no about two things at once – I believe that's essentially what we were doing when we got to numbers in the first place. We were getting to yes or no about a very broad category: is this a bird or not? And then getting to yes or no about how many birds: is this two birds or some other number? I guess that makes a per not only a relationship pair but a number as well."

"This is pretty amazing," Bruce interrupted. "You're telling us that the discovery of fractions, and the discovery that a fraction is a number, have their origins in bookkeeping – excuse me, in who x when recordkeeping? I'm afraid that most mathematicians are under the impression these discoveries came quite a bit later and were made by mathematicians."

Mrs. Thog smiled and resumed the story at the point where she had just asked Thog if they shouldn't name the two parts of each per, as long as they were at it. Thog thought the top number should be called a *numerator* – like a number – because it numbers or measures something, and the bottom one a *denominator* because it names – or nominates – what has been measured.

"Yes," Mrs. Thog said, "and rhyming as they do, it should be easy to remember that one always goes with the other."

At this point we took a break for lunch. During lunch, the discussion found its way from pers through ratios and all the way to the Greek philosophy that was based on rational numbers. The Greeks were pretty serious about their rational numbers. Apparently some friend of Thog's named Hippasus was put to death in 500 BC for discovering irrational numbers like "pi."*

"Some people believe it was Uncle Pi Thogarus who did him in," Thogette whispered to Bruce.

Like families everywhere, I guess even the Thogs have a few troublesome relatives.

---

*Irrational numbers have an infinite and nonrecurring expansion when expressed as a decimal. Examples are the square root of 2 and "pi," the ratio of the circumference of a circle to its diameter.

Chapter 31

The Discovery of Zero

As was politic, Chief Bear Ford picked right up on pers. As standard-setter, he assumed responsibility for them, renamed them "prices," and reconvened the elders to set "official prices." Chief Bear Ford explained that official prices would protect people from becoming the victims of "unfair prices." He took his official terminology pretty seriously, and holdouts who continued to secretly use the term "per" became known in official circles as "the who x when recordkeeping underground."

Mrs. Thog was among them. She began using pers in her who x when recordkeeping by writing each transaction bite as a per, designating bites for getting as plusses and those for giving as minuses. The numerator half of each per was generally beads, which, despite Chief Bear Ford's new coins of the realm, she still preferred using as money in her who x when work. It could be added to or subtracted from the numerator of any other per, even if the denominators differed. For example 10 beads that fetched 2 baskets of berries, and 20 beads that fetched 1 stone of mastodon could be added up as equal to 30 beads' worth. Of course, as Thog had pointed out earlier, adding up the 2 baskets of berries and 1 stone of mastodon as equal to 3 of something or other was less meaningful.

To make sure the who x when clearly showed getting and giving, Mrs. Thog marked the bite in the address for who got it with a plus and the bite in the address for who gave it up a minus. After recording bites in the who x when like this for a while, she noticed that if she added the numerators for all the plus bites and compared their sum with that of the numerators for all the minus bites, they were usually exactly the same number.

When she checked this out, she discovered that when the numerator plusses and minuses didn't add up to the same number, she had either made a mistake in writing down a per in the first place or in adding them up. After noticing and correcting such mistakes, the numerator plusses and minuses came out the same the next time she added them up.

She liked being able to check for recordkeeping mistakes like this, so she began double-checking her work on a regular basis. At first she did this by sorting the bites into two categories – one for plusses and one for minuses – and then adding both categories and comparing their sums. After a while she decided it would save sorting to simply add and subtract her way through the whos and whens, bite by bite. After all, the bites were designated with plusses and minuses, so they invited adding and subtracting.

But when she tried this, the pure sum of the numerators in the who x when came out to be nothing.

The idea of nothing wasn't too startling to Mrs. Thog. It

was like the idea of Thog going hunting and returning with nothing. Which had happened. Or it was like looking in a basket and finding no berries left: nothing. Which had happened. It was even a little like what she suspected that Junior did with much of his day: nothing – except daydream of tiger hunting, maybe.

Still, it seemed useful to have a name and a symbol for nothing, much as there were for other numbers like one, two, or three. This way she could write down the result of her arithmetic check much as she did when adding and subtracting other numbers. She decided to take all of this up with the family.

That night the Thogs listened attentively to Mrs. Thog's description of her recordkeeping day and the benefits of having a name and symbol for nothing – well, except for Junior, who was thinking about tiger hunting. But Thog and Thogette took seriously the challenge of figuring out just the right symbol for Mrs. Thog to use for nothing in her work.

Furrowing his brow while deep in thought, Thog took one of the new metal coins with Chief Bear Ford's picture on it and placed it on the ground. He looked at it, thinking, Hmm, money. Then he picked it up and looked at where it had been, thinking, Hmm, no money.

This finally caught Junior's attention and he exclaimed, "Why gosh, Dad, it's exactly like a tiger track! It leaves a little circle in the sand when it's gone, but you can tell it was there from the track."

"I think Junior has a point here," Thog said. "Why don't we take his suggestion?"

And to Mrs. Thog, he said, "As a symbol for nothing, perhaps you could use a 'track' – a little circle – to show that a number has been there once but isn't now."

"What will we call it, Daddy?" Thogette asked. "Not a 'track,' I hope!" (Thogette thinks hunting is yukky.)

After some thought, and mindful of Thogette's sensitivity, Thog said, "Why *zero*, I guess. At least it's a little shorter than nothing."

Well, let me tell you, the scientists were all thoroughly impressed by Mrs. Thog's discovery, and as the story ended Bruce said, "Say, Mrs. Thog, were you still in the Fertile Crescent when you discovered zero?"

"Why yes, we were."

"Wow! There goes traditional history out the window! Historians still think Brahmagupta discovered zero in AD 628."

"Oh, my," Mrs. Thog said.

"And they claim Bhaskara first applied negative numbers, exact equality, and zero to commercial recordkeeping in AD1180," he added.

"My goodness."

"Zero caught on rapidly because it enabled a more efficient positional numbering system as well as the development of modern mathematics and statistics."

Thogette gazed admiringly at Bruce.

"In fact," Jim said, "zero's now considered the most important tool of mathematics."

"It is pretty handy," Thog agreed.

"And Mrs. Thog discovered zero while balancing her books," Dr. Z enthused. "It's a bookkeeping discovery! And we still call the process she invented 'balancing the books.'"

"Yeah, Junior," I added (everyone else seemed to be getting more attention than him), "and you came up with a pretty cool symbol for it, too."

"Hey, thanks, man. Tracks are important to us hunter-gatherers."

Dr Z said, "Speaking of 'tracks,' I can just tell we're really on the track of the true meaning of debits and credits now."

Junior grinned at Dr. Z.

Mrs. Thog suggested we stop for dinner.

Chapter 32

The True Meaning of Debits and Credits

Dr. Z was right. We were on the trail to the true meaning of debits and credits. Right after dinner we tracked it down:

Zero turned out to be Chief Bear Ford's undoing. As standard-setter, he could never adjust to the idea that having responsibility for who x whens added up to responsibility for nothing.

Jim pointed out, in fairness to Chief Bear Ford, that zero is pesky, not like other numbers. If you add it to another number, that number stays the same, not budging, and exactly the same thing happens if you do the opposite and subtract it. But if you multiply any number by zero, it turns the number into zero, no matter what it was before. And, if you divide any number by zero, it turns the number into infinity, or everything possible, even if you're not sure exactly what infinity is. Jim thought arithmetic like this was probably pretty frustrating when you're trying to set standards!

Bruce pointed out that Chief Bear Ford had good company in his trouble with zero. Aristotle said there was no such thing, no infinity and no zero, and so did Archimedes. The Christians left it completely out of their calendar to prove it didn't exist. Later, after they learned to divide, they decided it did exist, because they liked the idea of infinity, but by then it was too late to change the calendar.

Dr. Z said that accountants love zero because they need it to balance their books.

Sasha observed that all this confusion over zero probably led to a spurt in membership in the who x when recordkeeping underground.

Thog confirmed that it did.

And the story continued: Mrs. Thog acquiescing, Thog and Junior finally went on their tiger hunt. Although she had agreed to it, Mrs. Thog still had misgivings about Junior tiger hunting. So to distract herself from worrying about him, she turned to her who x when recordkeeping with a vengeance, carefully keeping the bites balanced and equal to zero.

Zero proved a little tricky at first, even for Mrs. Thog, particularly when she multiplied or divided. But it also proved practical, just as she had envisioned it would. And like bookkeepers ever since, Mrs. Thog grew fond of it.

Thanks to zero she grew comfortable with the notion that for a bite to get into her records as a plus in the first place, she also had to enter a minus at the same time. A new minus seemed to linger behind each new plus.

But when Junior and Thog returned from their hunt a week later, aglow with satisfaction and dragging two dead tigers behind them, the last things on their minds were zero and this lingering minus. In fact, this minus nearly provoked a family incident, which Mrs. Thog only narrowly averted by a combination of extraordinary composure and the ability to think fast on her feet.

"I killed two tigers. They're huge! Aren't they magnificent, Mom?" Junior boasted, bursting with excitement.

Trying to think of exactly the right response for the occasion, Mrs. Thog said, "They look absolutely wonderful! And they sometimes fetch a nice per, you know."

"Oh, yes. I know!" Junior exclaimed, who understood that being sole owner of two tigers represented a big improvement over the meager allowance he got from his frugal parents.

"Perhaps," she suggested, "you would like to have your own who x when in honor of the occasion."

"Gosh, that would be great, Mom. Will you record these tigers for me?"

"Sure, I'll record plus two tigers and minus two tigers ..."

This stopped Junior cold, and his face clouded over. "Aw, come on, Mom, I'm plus two tigers, but not minus two. I'm not going to be minus these two tigers until I do something with them later!"

When Mrs. Thog said minus, it just plain hit Junior wrong.

Mrs. Thog was shocked. After all, it was Junior who'd suggested the symbol for zero! It took a minus to get to zero from a plus. What was going on here? But, she thought, he was probably more focused on the tiger-track aspects of zero than the arithmetic implications of the symbol itself. She decided you can't always expect logic from a teenager.

Plusses and minuses exactly described how things had moved from address to address in the real world during his hunt. There was a minus for every plus. Yesterday Thog and

Junior were dragging plus two tigers up the trail, and there were minus two tigers at the site of the kill. At the time of the kill, there were plus two dead tigers, and minus two live ones. For several hours before that, Junior and Thog were stalking plus two tigers, and there were minus two tigers wherever they had been before.

Mrs. Thog realized that thinking like this could go on and on – a journey back through a vast prior complexity. And getting into all this with Junior, when she was simply trying to make an entry in his who x when, would be a distraction. Junior was just not in the mood for a minus in his who x when!

Deep in thought, she hadn't said anything for a while, though she'd been looking right at Junior, and Junior knew better than to interrupt her when she appeared to be thinking about him.

Then Mrs. Thog had an idea. Turning to Thog she said sweetly, "You know, I never much liked these names, 'plus' and 'minus,' at least for who x when recordkeeping. I think Junior has a point here. The minus simply sounds wrong when the main idea is a plus."

The tension dissolved.

"But I do like using arithmetic in my who x when recordkeeping," she continued, "so perhaps, dear, you should name them something else, something a little softer and a little more ambiguous."

Thog was relieved that Mrs. Thog had so artfully dodged a prickly situation. He was also eager to get on with the tale of the hunt. After reflecting just a few seconds, he blurted: "Let's call the plus *debit* and the minus *credit*."

I know. These still sound funny – after all they'd perplexed Dr. Z since 1966 – but Thog didn't have very long to think them up.

Meanwhile, Thogette, who'd been viewing the tigers and considering how to paint them and in what light, looked up and said, "Daddy, what do those words mean that's different from 'plus' and 'minus'?"

"Oh, nothing, sweetie. But they have a nice ring and perhaps Junior will find them less troublesome than plusses and minuses."

It turned out Thog was right. Junior liked the idea of his mom debiting the tigers to his who x when and crediting him for the hunt.

And with this taken care of, they were able to get on with dinner and hear Thog and Junior's hunting story. Well, mostly they heard it from Junior, but Thog was able to get in a few words here and there.

And there you have it: the true meaning of debits and credits. The end of Dr. Z's quest. Another epiphany. By my count, this should be Dr. Z's third epiphany in our four days in the cave, and I expected her to be wildly enthusiastic about it, as she'd been about contracts and financial statements. But instead she just sat there in numb silence.

We all watched her.

Finally I said, "Well?"

Still silent, she looked crestfallen.

Then everyone jumped in, trying to make her feel better.

"Harumm," Thog said, clearing his throat, "the implications of plusses and minuses can be pretty paradoxical."

"Oh my, yes," agreed Mrs. Thog.

"Probably should have called it 'ambiguous economics' instead of 'quantum economics,'" said Bruce.

"Neils Bohr* did say the quantum can make you dizzy," Stu offered.

Sasha said, "Important things are often ambiguous."

Then Jim, "Science can be very exasperating."

A tear rolled down Dr. Z's cheek.

It was Junior who broke the ice. "Aw, c'mon, Dr. Z. You'll grow out of it. I did."

She started to laugh. Then she got the giggles. This went on for a while, causing the hiccups.

Mrs. Thog brought her a glass of water.

"Try drinking from it upside down," Jim suggested.

This finally did the trick.

---

* A quantum physicist and Nobel laureate.

Chapter 33

Half Is as Good as It Gets

The next morning at breakfast, most of the PartEcon team seemed restless; they wanted to get back to the laboratory. But Bruce thought the Thogs' story was about to take a scientific turn. Physicist's instinct, he explained. And Thogette suggested they stay a little longer, which may have influenced him. Anyhow, the story continued with all present:

After Chief Bear Ford fell over nothing, Chief Leaf assumed standard-setting duties.* Chief Leaf recognized the importance of maintaining who x when standards that were certain, and had the good sense to leave zero alone. He liked the sound of debits and credits and these became official terms, although being a big thinker he left the details of debits and credits to the elders. This earned him the nickname Chief Left It Be, which in time was shortened simply to Chief Left-It.

Chief Left-It began his reign by focusing on money and who had it, a tried-and-true approach among standard-setters. His first problem, of course, was to get the pictures

---

* Chief Leaf was named for his delicacy in handling strong forces like gravity. He seemed to have the ability, time after time, to float gently down from trees and land on his feet.

changed on all the coins of the realm, and this was no small undertaking, but he went right to work on it. When it came to money, he was a vigorous standard-setter, one who promised to be distracted by nothing. Chief Left-It soon grew more powerful than Chief Bear Ford had ever dreamed of being.

Meanwhile, the dinner celebrating Junior's first tiger hunt was a festive affair and the Thogs stayed up late. Mrs. Thog oohed and ahhed at all the right places each time the kill was recounted. Thogette, jealous of Junior again, reflected on how she might earn her own who x when someday. And Thog indulged in celebratory excess, imbibing certain agricultural derivatives prepared from one of Mrs. Thog's special recipes.

The next morning, while Thog slept on, Mrs. Thog took up her who x when recordkeeping. She needed to figure out how to deal with Junior's two tigers. She planned to record the tigers in two equal bites: one a plus, or debit; and, the other a minus, or credit. She decided to begin with the plus, since Junior was feeling positive.

Since this is Junior's who x when, she thought, from his perspective the tigers are mine, and the main thing here is to keep track of them for later, so I'll put the plus in the mine-later address.

As to the minus, she thought, hmm ... I should put this in mine-later as well, since from Junior's perspective they are mine. But now that we're using arithmetic, doing this will result in the mine-later address adding up to zero, and this might be too perplexing for the teenage mind.

Furthermore, she reflected, there's a practical problem with these debits and credits equaling zero. If both halves of a transaction are in exactly the same address, you can't measure the transaction at all. The arithmetic result is a zero.

	Now	Later
Mine	Mine Now:	Mine Later: + 2 Tigers - 2 Tigers 0 Tigers
Yours	Yours Now:	Yours Later:

Two Tigers Recorded in Junior's Who x When

She paused to ponder this. She didn't much like the idea of important things disappearing when she added them up. In the end she decided she needed some more precise addresses within the four addresses of the who x when to prevent this from happening.

If I put half of the transaction in one address and the other half in a different address, she thought, then adding the numbers in an address of the who x when doesn't remove those that I'm interested in.

She paused to consider this and eventually decided that the most you can know at any one time about any number in any particular address in the who x when is exactly half of the information about it. This seemed like an important principle: in who x when matters, there is no such thing as the whole story. Once you arrive at an address of interest, half is as good as it gets!

Mrs. Thog decided to prevail on Thog to name the general notion of a more precise address in the who x when, as well as the important principle she had discovered. And since she was anxious to show Junior his new who x when, she woke Thog up.

"Huh?" he said, groggily.

He's not at his best, she thought to herself.

"Umm ... dear, I was wondering about a name ..."

But before she could finish, he was fast asleep.

Mrs. Thog rolled her eyes in exasperation. Eager to get back to work, she decided to go ahead and name them herself. She decided to call the more precise addresses *accounts*. After all, there would undoubtedly be lots more accounts, and Thog would have the opportunity to name those. And she decided to call the principle she'd discovered the *half-is-as-good-as-it-gets principle*.

"Wow, the Heisenberg Uncertainty Principle!" Bruce exclaimed. "I <u>knew</u> something scientific would come up in this episode. Boy, there's a lot of physics in this who x when recordkeeping."

"The what?" Dr. Z asked.

"The principle in physics that we are simply never allowed all the information necessary to fully describe anything," Bruce said. "The most we are allowed to know about anything measurable is half, exactly half. As far as I know, nobody really knows why this is true, but if you accept the principle as a postulate, you get a theory that describes all known atomic phenomena."

"Here is an example that Lee Smolin, a gravitational physics friend of ours likes to use to explain the principle," Jim said. "A friend in Quantumland sends you a new pet in a quantum pet carrier. You may open only one end of the carrier at a time. So you open one end, and see the head of your new cat. Then you open the other end and see that you have a female. Next you recheck the other end, and this time it is the head of your dog. As you continue checking each end of the pet carrier, you discover that you may know either the sex of your new pet, or whether your pet is a dog or cat, but not both."

"Babylon Air regulations prohibit carry-ons containing undisambiguated pets."

"We understand that," Thogette replied politely, "Mom noticed the principle in the who x when and mentioned it to Uncle Thogenberg who thought it applied to a whole lot of other stuff as well. Finally, Heisenberg came along and proved it applied to everything in existence."

"Really?" Bruce asked. "Uncle Thogenberg? What a family you've got! Was Heisenberg a relative too?"

Thogette flashed him a fetching smile.

Accounts caught on and turned out to be quite a naming coup for Mrs. Thog. People who kept accounts went on to be known as "accountants," and their work to be known as "accounting."

As Mrs. Thog had foreseen, accounts also provided a veritable naming bonanza for Thog. In fact, that very night, more or less recovered from the prior evening's celebration, he named two accounts. The account in mine-later where Mrs. Thog had put Junior's plus-tiger bite, Thog named "Tigers" (which was later generalized to "inventories"). And, the mine-later account where she put the minus-tiger bite, he named "Equity."* But Mrs. Thog decided to defer discussion of the half-is-as-good-as-it-gets principle. Thog still didn't look his sharpest, and she knew it might seem a little paradoxical to someone with a muddled head.

With all this taken care of, Mrs. Thog was able to congratulate Junior at dinner, not only on his bravery and skill in

---

* In who x when recordkeeping for entities that are distinct from their owners, like corporations, accountants put equity in yours-later.

the hunt but also on his growing wealth as evidenced by his equity of two tigers! Junior was thrilled.

Thog went to bed early that night, leaving Mrs. Thog an opportunity to think more about Junior's who x when. Like moms everywhere she had high aspirations for her son, and she hoped he'd soon engage in commercial transactions involving commodities other than tigers. The commodity she had in mind was money.

But using money in Junior's who x when created a problem. What would she do about bites like his two tigers that didn't involve money yet? If a bite involved an inconsequential commodity she could just leave it out, but Junior hardly considered his tigers inconsequential. She needed to figure out how to assign a monetary measure to each of Junior's tiger bites to keep track of them in his who x when. Given Junior's sensitivity, she decided to talk this over with Thog in a private, parental kind of way at the next opportunity. Having decided this, Mrs. Thog called it a night, too.

We had to break for lunch. Up through the half-is-as-good-as-it-gets principle, we had the undivided attention of the entire PartEcon team, but as the story turned to recording this and that in Junior's who x when, they got restless. At lunch they announced plans to head back to the laboratory that very afternoon; they were eager to apply the Thogian breakthroughs to the collider. Thogette decided to go along with them, which seemed okay with her parents. After some discussion we all agreed that Thogette would use the Kurzweil converter, which I'd forgotten to bring with us to the cave, to keep a scientific record of what happened in the laboratory.

Dr. Z wanted to stay on in the cave and hear more about how one outgrows debits and credits. Thog and Mrs. Thog graciously agreed to tell her. I decided to stick with Thog, hoping to find out how his mastodon hunt with Ray had ended, and Junior decided to stick with us. He said he liked an occasional break from Thogette.

Chapter 34

Thogian Conservatism

After lunch, Thogette and the PartEcon team headed down the mountain with Stu in the lead, yodeling. Thog yodeled back, until the group disappeared from sight. Then he and Mrs. Thog and Junior got down to the serious business of trying to help Dr. Z outgrow debits and credits.

This is when, for who knows what reason, Dr. Z decided to inform the Thogs about one aspect of my past that I try to avoid emphasizing.

"Say, did you know that Brownie was once an accounting standard-setter himself?" she asked, out of the blue.

An uncomfortable silence followed.

Mrs. Thog came to my defense. "I'm sure you meant well, dear."

"That was a long time ago," I quickly pointed out. "Besides, the chief standard-setter ran me off and I've been underground ever since."

This broke the ice. Thog smiled and took up their story:

Coins of the realm were popular and Chief Left-It found maintaining a money standard relatively easy, despite a few coins here and there with the wrong picture on them and a few old-fashioned holdouts like the Thogs who were still exchanging beads instead of coins.

As for who x when standard-setting matters, Chief Left-It recognized the importance of the whole story and dismissed the half-is-as-good-as-it-gets principle as mumbo jumbo from the increasingly troublesome who x when recordkeeping underground. But he did embrace the new term "account," which sounded better than "half the information about a bite," and set the elders to work on determining official accounts for who x whens. Energetic Chief Left-It put them to work just two days after Junior's first tiger hunt.

"The half-is-as-good-as-it-gets principle is simply a rationalization for half-cooked books, another example of the dangerous nonsense being promulgated by criminals in the who x when recordkeeping underground."

—Chief Left-It (from his speech to the elders as quoted by the *Fertile Crescent Times*)

At the same time Thog and Mrs. Thog were also considering who x when matters. With Thogette indoors writing and Junior off mending fences and tending to his agriculture, Mrs. Thog got her chance to discuss the use of money in Junior's new who x when with Thog.

He listened carefully as she explained her thinking. "Wouldn't it be wise," she asked, "for Junior's who x when to accommodate more than tigers?"

Thog nodded in agreement. "You're absolutely right. Mastodon, for example."

"Actually, I was thinking more of money."

"Ah, yes. Money. That too, of course."

Mrs. Thog reminded him of the frisky nature of zero: if used as a numerator in Junior's tiger bites, the tigers would disappear completely, since zero divided by anything is still zero. They needed to come up with some sort of monetary numerator for his tiger bites for purposes of who x when recordkeeping.

They reviewed their who, when, and what alternatives. They considered when Junior might sell his tigers. Fresh tigers generally fetched more than riper ones, but then he might not sell the tigers at all, so not only when, but even if, was uncertain. They considered what the tigers might fetch, but then tigers might not fetch any of the amounts they came up with; it had been a while since there'd been a bona fide tiger transaction, so how much was uncertain. "And, if we put a prediction in his who x when now, we'll need to correct it continually," Mrs. Thog said. "Even with all of our simplifying inventions, this is still a cumbersome process."

They considered hedging their bet a little by assigning a

range of money measures to what the tigers might fetch, but applying arithmetic to any such range, along with all the other individual numbers in his who x when, would be difficult and impractical.

As they considered all this, they also worried about their credibility with Junior. "He has shown a healthy skepticism," Thog pointed out.

None of the alternatives seemed practical enough for the Thogs, and as Junior's anticipated return from his chores approached, Mrs. Thog said, "Maybe we should just assign a very small monetary measure to the tiger bites, one that won't be confused with a prediction but will preserve their existence in the who x when."

And this is what they decided to do. They also decided it would be nice to name this minimal measure. Thog suggested calling such amounts *nominal*.

To avoid confusing nominal measures with uncertain predictions of what things might fetch, Mrs. Thog thought they should also name the predictions themselves. Thog thought the term "predictions" too didactic and suggested calling them *guesses* instead.

"Come to think of it," Mrs. Thog said, "I suppose we should also have a name for the general approach to who x when recordkeeping – a name that conveys our not getting too far ahead of things and using nominal numbers instead of guesses in our who x when."

"Well," Thog said, after a moment, "what if we called it *conservatism*? It's not an original name, but perhaps using a popular term will convey the main idea."

"Conservatism is a nice name," she replied, "and you

are wise to borrow names occasionally. If we have too many original ones, our vocabulary will become jargon rather than a discipline."

"Oh yes," Dr. Z piped up, when it appeared the Thogs had finished naming things. "Conservatism caught on. Many still consider it the cornerstone of good accounting."

Chapter 35

Profits

Chief Left-It embraced the term "conservative," promising to take conservative steps to protect who x whens. But he hated the term "guesses." After all, standards are supposed to give people a feeling of certainty, he said. So guesses joined half-is-as-good-as-it-gets and pers, relegated to the who x when recordkeeping underground.

The underground was beginning to annoy Chief Left-It, and he decided it was time to crack down and clean it up. As a first step, he ruled that any remaining beads, whether or not they competed with coins as money, were to be kept veiled and out of sight.

Chief Left-It also decided that official prices should represent the next trade that might occur, not the last one that really did, and be called "fair values," which he said made who x whens more reliable for their users.

Meanwhile, the Thogs had no sooner decided what to do about Junior's tigers in his who x when than he walked in. And the first words out of his mouth were, "Hey, Mom, last night you mentioned my growing wealth. How much money do you think my tigers might fetch?"

"Why not ask your father," she said.

"Ahem ..." Thog opined. "I guess they might fetch anywhere from 300 to 500 beads, depending, of course, upon a number of factors. Meanwhile, your mother is keeping them in your who x when at the nominal value of one bead each."

"Beads?" said Junior, who keeps up with political developments. "How much is that in coins?"

"It's been a while since there was a bona fide tiger transaction, but I think the last one was in beads," Thog said.

"Anyhow," Mrs. Thog chimed in, "when you do sell your tigers, you may show a handsome *profit.* What that profit might turn out to be is just a guess, and of course your who x when won't reflect a guess. It will only reflect a profit when you actually have one. This, of course, is only *proper.*"*

Junior asked, "Like, what's this 'profit' stuff, Mom?" (He knew what proper meant.)

Thog, who hadn't heard the term "profits" before, either, listened attentively to her answer.

"Profit is simply the difference between the mine-now and the yours-now cells in your who x when."

Although he'd been distracted by a minus the day before, Junior was not unfamiliar with arithmetic, and now he did some in his head. "I see. My profit might equal 500 beads minus the one-bead nominal cost you used for keeping track of my tiger, or 499 beads. You're right, Mom, that would be a swell profit!"

---

* Propriety was then, as it is now, oft invoked by both moms and accountants.

"It's just a guess," Thog cautioned.

"Yes, yes, I know," Junior said.

As Junior left, and just out of his hearing, Thog said to Mrs. Thog: "That was quick thinking, dear, that profit arithmetic. And what a nice name you chose – 'profit,' I mean."

Mrs. Thog smiled. "Why, thank you, dear, but without your conservatism there might not be any profit when Junior sells his tigers."

Junior awoke the next morning with profit on his mind, so he decided to go to the market and see what his tigers might fetch. He came home whistling that afternoon. In place of one of his tigers, he had 400 beads in his pouch and a clay tablet indicating he was owed 100 more at a later date.

"Hey, Mom," he called out, "I sold one of my tigers already. I got 500 beads, the high end of Dad's guess, although I had to take a tablet for 100 beads, which I won't get paid until later." And he proudly unveiled his beads and displayed his tablet for her to see.

"Will you record this in my who x when?"

"Of course, dear," Mrs. Thog said.

Ever since Mrs. Thog invented accounts, Thog had been busy naming various new accounts, so Junior's who x when included accounts in mine-later called "tigers," "cash," "accounts receivable," and "equity"; as well as "revenues" in mine-now, and "expenses" in yours-now. And Mrs. Thog had already recorded Junior's tigers in terms of nominal beads (using pers, of course).

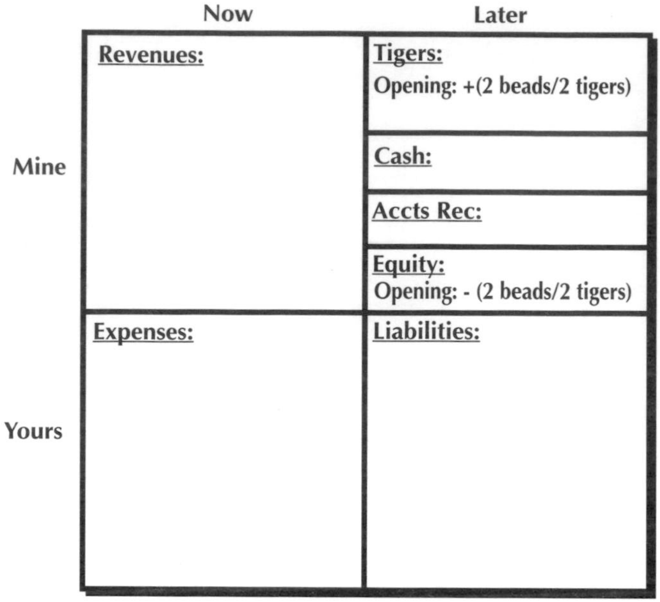

	Now	Later
Mine	**Revenues:**	**Tigers:** Opening: +(2 beads/2 tigers)
		Cash:
		Accts Rec:
		Equity: Opening: - (2 beads/2 tigers)
Yours	**Expenses:**	**Liabilities:**

Junior's Who x When

When Mrs. Thog began describing how she'd recorded Junior's tiger sale in his who x when, Dr. Z asked if she could make the entry herself.

"Why, of course, dear."

Dr. Z whipped another sharpened pencil from her backpack. (She offered one to me, but I decided to just bluff my way through.) And then, licking her pencil, she went to work. She recorded the tiger sale in five steps: First, she recorded the bite representing the 400 beads Junior had already received in cash. Second, she recorded the 100 beads due him in accounts receivable. She marked these both "plus," reassuringly saying "debit" aloud. Third, she recorded the bite representing the 500-bead sum of these two plusses in revenues, marking it "minus" (and saying "credit"). Fourth, she removed from assets a bite representing the monetary equivalent of one of his tigers, since the actual tiger was gone. The Thogs had given the bite a nominal numerator of one bead, and Dr. Z used a minus to remove this from the tiger account. And fifth, she recorded a corresponding plus in expenses.

	Now	Later
Mine	Revenues: Step 3: - (500 beads/1 tiger)	Tigers: Opening: + (2 beads/2 tigers) Step 4: - (1 bead/1 tiger) Total: + (1 bead/1 tiger) Cash: Step 1: + (400 beads/1 bead) Accts Rec: Step 2: + (100 beads/1 bead) Equity: Opening: - (2 beads/2 tigers)
Yours	Expenses: Step 5: + (1 bead/1 tiger)	Liabilities:

Junior's Who x When After Tiger Sale

"Is that how you did it?" she asked Mrs. Thog.

"Exactly."

Mrs. Thog resumed her story. Checking on his who x when, Junior said, "Hey, Mom, how's my profit look?"

"It's just as you figured yesterday, dear. Five hundred beads revenue minus one bead expense, or 499 beads profit."

"Great." And off Junior went, smiling and thinking of how best to lord it over his sister with his new who x when and the personal wealth it represented. Profit, he thought to himself, is a good thing!

As it turned out, Thogette had overheard this conversation. She's a thoughtful girl, and there was something about it that didn't seem quite right to her, but she couldn't put her finger on it right then. She decided to keep quiet until she figured it out.

Chief Left-It, on the other hand, didn't keep quiet until he figured out either profits or propriety. Instead he proclaimed that the elders would begin work immediately on setting standards for proper profits in who x when recordkeeping, and standard-setters have been at it ever since.

Chapter 36

Banking in Santa Fe

The PartEcon team and Thogette spent most of the afternoon walking down the mountain, and by the time they arrived in Santa Fe they were tired. Although Thogette was eager to see the particle collider, they decided to wait until morning to go to the laboratory.

The PartEcon men were wondering where Thogette should stay, but before they'd finished discussing it she'd checked into the best hotel in town. And after speaking briefly with the clerk, the manager appeared to make sure everything was exactly as she wished.

"Yes, ma'am, we hope your stay with us meets your expectations." He smiled and bowed.

"It appears that you've done this before," said Stu, who is usually unflappable but was surprised at this.

"Oh my, yes," Thogette said over her shoulder as she headed for her room.

But that wasn't the half of it. When the PartEcon men returned an hour later to pick her up in the hotel lobby for dinner, she was wearing just the right denim clothing with silver accents, and looked as though she'd stepped straight from a fashion article on Santa Fe haute couture.

Bruce was a bit flabbergasted, but warming to the occasion he suggested they go to the best French restaurant in town. Ensconced at the table, Thogette studied the menu and then ordered: Paté de Lapin, Aile de Raie aux Capres, Pommes Vapeur, Gratinée de Coquilles St. Jacques and, Salade d'Endives, Noix au Roquefort – all in flawless French and with the courses in the right order, too. There was one tricky moment when Bruce suggested a bottle of Chateau-Figeac premier grand cru classe de Saint-Emilion and Thogette got carded. Apparently the waiter was confused by the BC on her ID, but Thogette finessed this by sniffing the cork and hinting a frown, and before you knew it the waiter was fawning over her just as the hotel manager had done.

Bruce interrupted Thogette's colloquy with the waiter by saying, "Uhh, I'd thought that eating here might be something of a new experience – for a hunter-gather, I mean."

"Oh not at all," she replied (in English for Bruce's benefit). "One does this sort of thing in banking all the time."

"You're a banker?"

"Oh yes. At least I was for a time. I could explain, but it would involve another episode in our family story."

"Please tell us," Bruce said.

Thogette said that she'd been thinking for quite a while about a who x when of her very own, and finally she got an idea while she and Junior were talking.

"Junior is basically the denominator type," she explained. "He likes physical stuff – particularly when it comes to his money. We were disagreeing about money. He thought it was concrete and I thought it was just an idea."

Thogette had noticed that the neighboring

Mesopotamians were storing people's physical money, and she reasoned that they were using who x whens to keep a record of what they were storing. Her idea was to take this a step further and replace physical money with what she decided to call "arithmetic money." After all, physical money got dirty when you handled it, was cumbersome to carry around, and was easy to lose.

She would need a who x when, of course. And, as in any who x when, she would use bites, representing each by a per. The per's numerator represented money's measurement aspect and the per's denominator represented its transaction aspect. This meant that other people could deposit and spend their money if she simply did the arithmetic for them in her own who x when.

She explained: "When people deposited their money with me, I just put a plus in my who x when in mine-later showing that I had custody of it, and a minus in yours-later showing they had the same money because I owed it to them. And then when they wanted to spend their money, it just worked the other way around."

"If there's a record of money," she continued, "then you don't need the physical stuff."

She said the family liked her idea a lot and Thog thought it should be named *banking*, a shorter and catchier name than "Thogette's Who x When for Just Money."

Thog pointed out that scaling up a model like banking and producing actual physical results could take a little time, and he warned Thogette to be patient. As he predicted, it did take a while, but eventually her invention caught on.

"Scaling things up commercially," Thogette explained,

"is like modeling in the other direction. In modeling you make big, complicated things simpler so you can understand them. In scaling up, you start with a simple model and get more people participating. The next thing you know, you have a full-scale enterprise."

Bruce said, "Not long after banks began taking deposits and lending money in the Fertile Crescent, banks also sprang up in Athens, Rome, and elsewhere. But I didn't realize they created money just by using arithmetic."

"Well, I'm afraid that's all there is to it," Thogette said. "That's exactly how they do it, although nowadays it takes a few more entries for reserve requirements and whatnot."

"Your idea must have been a little ahead of the times," Bruce said. "Didn't gold, copper, and silver also continue to serve as physical money for a number of years after there were banks?"

"Well, some things take a while," she said philosophically. "But in 1971, the President of the United States did finally abandon the gold standard, accepting that money is actually just a record of an idea."

"Why do you suppose it took so long?" Jim asked.

"Well, presidents do like having their pictures on the coin of the realm."

Chapter 37

Closing the Who x When

Bright and early the next morning those of us in the cave heard how despite all the Thogs' simplifying inventions, complexity was still a problem. After sticks, tokens, and bullae came clay tablets, and now there were too many of these. Clay tablets were stacked everywhere, and once again things had become a real mess around the cave. Sometimes it seemed to Mrs. Thog that when it came to complexity, her work was never done.

Well, she thought, the who x when is organized by "up-to-now"* and "later." Perhaps I could just keep a summary of the numerators and get rid of some of the older denominators.

She considered this for a while and decided on a plan: She would keep the tablets for both the numerators and denominators of the bites in the "later" addresses in her who x when. She would need these in the future to complete the transactions they represented. But she wouldn't keep all the tablets in the "up-to-now" addresses. After all, by now there was nearly 7,000 years' worth of stuff there. She would start

---

*This is because a series of entries in the "now" cells of a who x when ends up representing transactions "up-to-now."

eliminating some of these in an orderly way. Beginning with the oldest, she would discard them one millennium at a time. After 6,000 years, she would discard things a hundred years at a time. During the latest hundred years, she would discard things ten years at a time. And during the last ten years, she would discard things one year at a time.

In the future, she would continue discarding things once a year, which seemed about right for who x when recordkeeping and would be easy to remember to do, since it dovetailed nicely with her gardening schedule.

To summarize what she'd discarded, she would use a single number – profit or loss – that simply represented the arithmetic sum of the numerators before each date in the disposal sequence. And she would keep track of these profit summaries and the periods they represented "for later" in the account called "equity."

Mrs. Thog began her task with the summarizing work, and let me tell you, summarizing 7,000 years' worth of old denominators took a lot of arithmetic! In fact, when Mrs. Thog was only partway through the task, she told herself, "This makes berry counting look like a picnic." (Here, in an aside to us she explained that this is one reason she was so excited to learn about computers from Dr. Kurzweil.)

She'd made it all the way up to the prior decade in the "up-to-now" cells when suddenly she remembered she needed to double-check her math for zero using the "later" cells of the who x when, to make sure she hadn't made any mistakes.

"Oh, confound it," she thought, "I should have been doing this year by year. It would have been so much easier that way. I sure hope this thing is going to balance now." And holding her breath, Mrs. Thog proceeded to check the entire who x when.

She was lucky. All the numerators balanced exactly to zero on the first try.

"Whew, what a relief!" she sighed. "The thought of redoing all that arithmetic was more than I could bear. I'll be more careful from here on out."

Then she thought, as long as she planned to balance the entire who x when year by year like this, why not prepare a summary of it at the same time?

And when she did she got the annual financial statements that Dr. Z had had an epiphany about during the who x when episode: an income statement that measured what happened the year before, and a balance sheet that measured what remained to be completed later.

Thog thought they should call this summarizing process *closing the who x when.*

"A good choice, dear," Mrs. Thog said. "If we call it 'cleaning up the cave,' I'm afraid the children will resist participating."

As this episode concluded, Dr. Z remarked: "When you invented what accountants now call 'closing the books,' or 'periodic financial reporting,' I believe you were applying the same principles you used when you invented counting, standards, arithmetic, and money. You were simplifying complexity by shearing away unnecessary detail, keeping only a single number, a yes-or-no measure, that represented a variety of pers that were interesting once but lost relevance with the passage of time."

"Why, yes, of course," Mrs. Thog said.

"Nowadays accountants have to be a little careful what they throw away," I commented.

"Yes they do," Thog grumbled.*

"Cave cleaning was a troublesome concept for Chief Left-It," Mrs. Thog explained. "He decided that closing who x whens offered a good opportunity to develop more standards and he announced that all who x whens were to be closed annually and reflect proper profits. Then he came up with what he called 'taxes.' These, he proclaimed, would be assessed annually based on profit that reflected fair values. And to be certain that everything was fair and proper and everyone had paid all their taxes, nothing was to be thrown away – ever. I'm sure he meant well, but he did somehow miss one of the main points of cave cleaning."

"And taxes weren't that popular either," Thog concluded.

---

*The SEC has accused the Thogs of shredding tablets from 46,000 BC to 2000 BC in an attempt to obfuscate their true motives at the time of certain of their alleged inventions.

Chapter 38

Outgrowing Debits and Credits

Before lunch we heard about how Junior handled Dr. Z's problem of outgrowing debits and credits.

Junior had been bragging about his who x when, which annoyed Thogette, so she turned her attention to various ways she might torment him. She decided on arithmetic as her weapon.

Thogette noticed that people seemed to think of both their assets and their profits as plusses; at least that's how they talked about them. She felt sure that Junior, too, thought like this. She had heard him say that profits equaled revenues minus expenses, and this had been bothering her.

When Junior sold his tigers they were subtracted from assets and added to expenses, causing his expenses, generally considered minuses, to be represented by plusses. Moreover, when he sold his tigers his money was added to assets, which required, for balance, subtracting it from revenues, causing his revenues to be minuses. All of which meant that Junior's profits were minuses, and any losses were plusses. And this just had to be the opposite of how Junior thought of them!

Junior may be a little thick, she thought, but he can add and subtract, and if this doesn't just devastate him, nothing will!

Writing on a fresh clay tablet, she constructed a conceptual plus-and-minus model of a who x when. She decided to title her model "Any Who x When," rather than "Junior's Who x When." This would suggest an innocent motive, so he'd never suspect that she was trying to bring him down a notch.

	Now	Later
Mine	Revenues -	Assets +
Yours	Expenses +	Liabilities -
	Profits - Losses +	

Thogette's Model of Any Who x When

That night, smiling sweetly, Thogette brought her model in to dinner. When the moment seemed right, she introduced the topic of her general plus-and-minus model of any who x when, and everyone listened politely.

But somehow Thogette had misjudged things. She'd showed conclusively that profits are minuses; there was no question about that. "But after all, sweetie, you could reverse all the signs in the who x when and it would still work just as well," her father said.

"Why, yes," Mrs. Thog said, "it's just a convention – changing the signs."

And to make matters worse, Junior, rather than coming completely unglued, said, "Gosh, I think I like using plusses and minuses better than debits and credits anyhow. It makes a lot of sense to put a minus on an abstract idea like my revenues, and to have the plus on something concrete like my actual cash. I mean, after all, revenue is only an idea."

Thogette blurted, "Well, Junior, so is money. Money's just an idea, too, you know!"

Then she stopped to listen to what she'd just said. She barely heard Junior complimenting her on her model and her thoughtfulness about arithmetic. She realized she'd just had her Big Idea – the one for her own who x when. But given the way things were going, she kept it to herself that evening.

So this is how Junior stumped Thogette by outgrowing debits and credits when she least expected it.

"That's what accountants do, you know," Dr. Z said. "They reverse half the signs when they prepare financial statements so readers aren't confused by the arithmetic. In fact, there are rules requiring public companies to do it."

"Really – rules against arithmetic?" Mrs. Thog said.

"No wonder we're back to hunting rabbits," Thog groused.

"Well, I think we're finished with this episode, dear,"

said Mrs. Thog.

We all looked at Dr. Z to see how she was coming along.

She blushed and said: "Thank you all so very much. I do believe I have finally outgrown debits and credits myself." (This was now her fourth epiphany, in case you're counting.)

"See Dr. Z," Junior said, "I told you. There's nothing to it, really!"

Well, she thought, nothing but quantum decoherence, binaries, combinatorics, matrices, equality, zero, and whatnot, but instead she said: "Yes, the paradox of nothing would appear to sum it up."

"I suppose now we should head down to the laboratory and see if we can help out there," Thog said.

"We can leave anytime," Mrs. Thog said. "I've packed a basket lunch."

"Then let's go," Dr. Z said, relieved to be out of the limelight.

Chapter 39

Colliding with What x Whats

The PartEcon team and Thogette arrived at the secret laboratory about the same time that Dr. Z outgrew debits and credits at the cave. Thogette got a lab coat and a tour of the lab, as well as an opportunity to inspect the particle collider and review the schematic and instrumentation diagrams. She also checked out the Kurzweil converter, which, like most of Ray's inventions is intuitive and easy to use. But what seemed to impress her most was the organ, which was still playing Bach.

"The music is lovely, but why an organ here in the laboratory?" she asked.

"Security precaution. It covers the collider hum," Jim said. "Plus Bruce likes it. He plays, you know – gives concerts on Sundays."

"Oh Bruce, you will play for me sometime, won't you?"

"Y-y-yes," Bruce stammered, blushing.

"OK," Thogette said, rubbing her hands together and getting back to business. "Now I'll just turn on the converter as I promised I would. Where do you suggest we start?"

Stu: Perhaps we should begin with a brief review to refocus ourselves. (all nod in agreement) Well, on the particle front, we begin with the most basic possible things: particles, represented by symbol strings constructed from bits, which the particle loader sends into the collider.

Sasha: Then the Lego™ possibilities generator identifies random possibilities for particle combinations, which collide with the particles in the collider.

Bruce: And when an actual individual particle collides with a possibility that includes it, an agent occurs for that possibility.

Thogette: I see. When they collide, are you using pers to represent the possibilities?

Jim: Fractions?

Thogette: Yes, or you probably think of them as pairs. From an agent's perspective they occur together – particles paired with possibilities for them.

Sasha: But to begin with, there's just one physical particle.

Thogette: Actually, I think there's one physical particlein the loader and the idea of a particle in the possibilities generator. These come together when an agent is created. One physical particle represented as a per would be one unit of measure over one unit of the idea of that particle. If there is more than one physical particle – say, three – then there'd be three in the measuring numerator over one unit of the idea, or three physical particles. But any way you look at it, it's still a pair, or a per.

Jim: Ah yes, there is the idea of each particle as well as the particle itself.

Thogette: I believe so.

Bruce: You know, you're right, of course. (to the others) You heard her. Let's get the pers in there.

Sasha: OK, what else?

Thogette: Well, in order to learn from its own experience, each agent will need a unique record, which will expand with its individual experience. So each agent will need a what x what.

Stu: She's absolutely right. We discussed this in the cave.

Thogette: Perhaps I can help with the what x whats. Mom's better at this stuff than I am, but I'll give it a whirl.

Jim: OK, I'll code, and maybe you wouldn't mind watching over my shoulder in case I get off track?

Thogette: Sure.

(all watch over Jim's shoulder as he codes the collider to represent each particle possibility as a pair in the collision code and gives each agent its own what x what)

Thogette: Looks right to me. If we have it, the what x what should expand for each agent each time it encounters a new per in haggle.

Jim: Shall we give it a try?

Bruce: (gets out the safety gear) OK. But give me a sec to get this set up. We still gotta be careful here.

(all undergo standard collider drill)

Sasha: (watches the macro monitor) Ura! Ura!

Jim: What?

Sasha: Ooops. Wrong language. I became overexcited. I meant Hurray! Would you look at this? We have what looks like money emerging! Look at this graph! Oh, there is hope, there is hope after all!

Jim: Yep. Looks like those pers are doing the trick.

Thogette: Shouldn't there be two graphs – one for transaction money and one for measurement money? (pauses) Oh my goodness, can you believe it? We forgot the agent who x whens. How silly of me!

(Jim stops the collider and codes up a who x when for each agent)

Thogette: I can't believe I forgot the who x whens! Anyhow, that should do it. Now we should see the measurement money emerge as the agents begin using the same currency for transacting and as a measure to keep their who x whens. I heard on the street that nowadays accountants call this kind of measurement money a firm's "functional currency."

(Jim restarts the collider)

Stu: (watches the macro monitor) Ah yes, look. There are two graphs for emergent currencies now – one for measurement and one for transacting.

Sasha: Ura! Ura! Ura! Emergent money!

(all watch collider run)

Sasha: (watches the agent monitor) Uh-oh, we're running out of consumers again. Look here. (points)

(all study the monitor)

Jim: (turns off collider) Hey, let's turn this thing off and think about this consumer problem some more. Besides, it's a good time for a break.

Bruce: Thogette, thank you very much. You have certainly been a wonderful help so far!

Thogette: Perhaps not. The collider doesn't seem to be working very well yet. We can't just keep adding consumers, can we?

Sasha: Not really–at least not if we want to be scientific about things.

Stu: Well, let's go somewhere for lunch and discuss the biology of the possibilities generator. In my view, we've made quite good progress here this morning, and in science it's important to stop from to time and savor your progress, discussing things over a nice meal with your colleagues.

Chapter 40

Agent Metabolism

It didn't take Dr. Z and me long to hike down the mountain into Santa Fe with the Thogs. They set a brisk pace, and I got a break because both Thog and Junior offered to carry Dr. Z's immense backpack. Junior ended up with it and bounded along as if it were weightless. The Thogs were quite the naturalists and entertained us with their knowledge of plants, animals, and – of course – tracks.

The time flew by, and before we knew it we were heading up the road to the secret laboratory. There, coming toward us, was the PartEcon team and Thogette, on their way back from lunch.

After we exchanged enthusiastic greetings, Jim recounted their dinner last night at the restaurant and summarized Thogette's banking story for those of us who had missed it.

"Banking must have been Thogette's Big Idea," Dr. Z said.

"Yes it was," Thogette confirmed.

"And Dr. Z," Sasha asked, "how did it go – outgrowing debits and credits?"

Dr. Z blushed. "Uhh, fine. How did it go in the laboratory?" she asked to change the subject.

"Well," Stu reported, "we made substantial progress this morning – scientifically speaking – thanks, I must say, to Thogette. We have some emergent money now – with a power-law flavor – in two dimensions. But we're still having some sticky problems with the possibilities generator. Consumer problems. In fact, Thog, now that you're here, perhaps we can review our Fibonacci mathematics one more time."

"Ah yes," Thog said. "Rabbits and economic troubles seem to go hand in hand. Fibonacci knew what he was doing when he selected rabbits to illustrate combinatorics. In political accounting circles he was known as Leonardo. But in the who x when recordkeeping underground, we called him Fibonacci."

"Leonardo wrote the first known book on double-entry accounting," Dr. Z said. "Some accounting historians consider him the father of accounting, but of course they don't know about Mrs. Thog."

Mrs. Thog blushed.

"What a coincidence! The same guy, with different names, was both the father of combinatoric statistics and the father of accounting," Bruce said. "I guess accounting and combinatorics have gone together for a long time."

"I bet that Fibonacci's not the only member of the who x when recordkeeping underground who used an alias," Sasha said.

"Why, no, he wasn't," Thog said.

"Did you ever have an alias?" I asked Thog.

"Naah, I just stayed as far away as possible from politics."

"Tell us about Fibonacci alias Leonardo, then," Dr. Z said.

"Well," said Mrs. Thog, "I became interested in Fibonacci because Thog and I had a little – I believe you call it – epiphany of our own."

"Oh my!" Dr. Z exclaimed, relieved not to be the only one having epiphanies. "You must tell us about it as soon as we get to the lab."

After Thog, Mrs. Thog, and Junior had toured the lab and looked over the collider and schematics, Thogette turned on the converter and we sat down to hear about Thog and Mrs. Thog's epiphany.

Mrs. Thog: Well, let's see. Where were we? It was Junior who pointed it out to us.

Dr. Z: Pointed out what?

Thog: What I believe you now call "statistics."

Bruce: Really?

Junior: (whispers to Jim) You know I've already heard this stuff. Would you mind if I tinkered with the collider while you guys go through it one more time? Your model is the coolest of the cool and I'm having trouble keeping my hands off of it. I'll listen with one ear, in case something comes up.

Jim: (whispers) Sure, go ahead. Be a little careful–you know combinatorics, and all. Oh, and be sure not to hit the green collide button.

Junior: (whispers) Thanks. I'll be careful.

Mrs. Thog: You see, after Junior sold his two tigers, he began looking for more denominators for his who x when, and he decided to try his hand at wheel-making.

Thog: Back in those days, he was using wood, of course.

Mrs. Thog: As I recall, he purchased 5 stones of wood for 100 beads, enough for a first wheel, allowing for scrap and whatnot. Of course, he recorded this in his inventory as +100 beads/ 5 stones of wood. His first wheel was a nice one, which he sold for 300 beads and recorded as +300 beads in cash and -300 beads in revenues. Then he set about to compute his profit. To do this he had to measure the wood in inventory from which he'd built his wheel. And this is when he encountered the problem that wheels for sale were measured in beads/wheel, whereas wood for construction was measured in beads/stone.

Thog: Junior puzzled over how to account for the sale of his wheel. He could just divide his 100-bead purchase by 5 stones, making the 3 stones of wood he'd used worth 60 beads, but the wood he had left in inventory wasn't quite as nice as the wood he'd used to build that first wheel, so this didn't make sense. He could charge the full 100 beads he had paid for the wood against the first wheel, but he planned to make another wheel, and this would leave the remaining wood carried at 0 monetarily, which he would then lose track of in his who x when, so this didn't make sense, either.

Mrs. Thog: This is when Junior realized, and pointed out to us, that there are judgmental choices involved in measuring profit on the physical transformation of denominators, none of which is completely certain.

Thog: In the end he decided to lean in a conservative direction, charging all but 2 beads of the original 100-bead wood purchase against the first wheel. This improved his chance to compute a profit on the completion and sale of a second wheel. He carried his remaining wood inventory at a nominal amount to keep track of it in his who x when, just as we did with his first two tigers.

Dr. Z: Accountants call this "cost accounting." But I thought your epiphany had to do with statistics.

Mrs. Thog: Yes, dear, I'm coming to that. Anyhow, Thog named the physical changes that occasioned changes in the units of measurement *transformations*. He thought transformations were important, because they reminded him of eating. I thought, What? But he explained that it's because eating can go both ways. You can eat a tiger or you can be eaten. Of course he was right. It can go both ways. Transformations are directional.

Junior: (shouts, interrupts) Hey guys, I've got it! I know what's wrong with your possibilities generator! You've only got one transformation direction in here.

Stu: (exclaims at full professorial volume, simultaneous with Junior's shout) I know what's wrong with the biology in the possibilities generator now. We're only constructing possibilities. But it's like metabolism – it should go both ways. We need deconstructive metabolisms as well.

Jim: Wait a minute here. Everyone's talking at once. How am I gonna code whatever's going on here?

(all talk at once)

Mrs. Thog: (sternly) One at a time, please!

(complete silence)

Mrs. Thog: (formally) Ahem ... Dr. Kauffman, I believe you were trying to tell us something about biology.

Stu: Excuse me, Mrs. Thog, yes I was. Deconstructive metabolisms in biology occur when one measure is broken down into two or more, as happens when you eat something and it becomes various parts of you.

Mrs. Thog: (sterner than with Stu) And Junior, although I don't think you've been listening at all, you too were trying to say something?

Junior: Aw, Mom, give me a break. I was just saying they don't have any transformations in here that go the other way. They have everyone making one thing out of two, and no one making two things out of one.

Sasha: (loud and out of the blue) That's what consumers do – they eat! Deconstructive metabolisms are consumers!

Mrs. Thog: (less sternly) I believe we can hear you, Sasha. We're sitting quite close.

Sasha: (subdued) Oh, I'm sorry, Mrs. Thog. I meant to say that's why we aren't getting consumers, economically speaking – because of the metabolisms, or transformations, or whatever they are not being bi-directional.

Mrs. Thog: Yes, well I understand it would be nice to have some more consumers in the model, but perhaps it would be best if we took this a step at a time so Jim has some idea of how to code it.

Dr. Z: Mrs. Thog, was bi-directional transformations your epiphany?

Mrs. Thog: Not yet, dear.

Jim: I think this one was ours.

Junior: Well, let's see, the first thing about a transformation – what you call a metabolism – is that an agent representing an entire transformation cannot be in all of its possible transformation states at the same time.

Jim: Of course. If an agent makes omelets from eggs and cheese, then he can have eggs, he can have eggs and cheese, or he can have an omelet. But after the eggs and cheese are an omelet, they aren't eggs and cheese anymore. So an agent omelet-maker can't be in all these states at once.

Thogette: I believe that's how the collider works now. When a particle possibility first encounters a particle included in that possibility, an agent occurs that is essentially in one of the states you're describing.

Jim: That's right.

Thogette: The idea-half of the particle pair completes an agent's metabolic thought, of course. So if an agent has eggs, its physical state is eggs, plus the idea of cheese and the idea of combining cheese and eggs for an omelet – all represented by pers.

Junior: Actually that was <u>my</u> idea.

Mrs. Thog: (sternly) Children!

Thog: It's like one of Mrs. Thog's recipes – what I think <u>you</u> call an "equation": 12 eggs + 1 pound of cheese = 1 (large) omelet. If you like large omelets, as I do, you may enjoy the omelet more than the arithmetical sum of its parts – hence the possibility for profits.

Stu: Nothing like a little basic biology to bring things together.

Mrs. Thog: Or a good recipe to facilitate trade.

Thog: Or a really good omelet!

Dr. Z: (grows excited once again) It's the profit equation, of course!

Jim: What?

Dr. Z: The recipe. The one in the box. I mean, if you turn it around it is. For example: omelets sold (in money) – the cost of eggs (in money) - the cost of cheese (in money) = profit.

Mrs. Thog: (to Dr. Z) Why yes, dear, of course.

Dr. Z: Was this the epiphany? The accounting equation?

Mrs. Thog: No dear. We haven't quite come to it yet.

Jim: I think I can put the correct transformation code in the possibilities generator now.

Dr. Z: OK, but I want to hear about the Thogs' epiphany first.

Chapter 41

Measuring In-Betweens

Junior enjoyed reporting his profits to the family, Mrs. Thog said, and he accompanied his reports with long explanations of how he'd measured the various transformations involved in computing his profits. But Thogette complained about Junior's reports. His profit seemed to her to be too precise a number to summarize something so complex that it required a long explanation.

This set Junior to thinking about the yes or nos involved in measuring his transformations. He decided to use Thogette's arithmetic, hoping to catch her out in a mistake so he could explain his measurements to her in terms of her own invention.

To begin with he decided to write yes or no like this: "Yes = 1; No = 0." Then he thought about making wheels. One day he bought the wood; the next, he got up early and began working. It took him about a day to build a wheel; and, on the third day, he took the wheel to market and sold it as one unit of wheels.

He thought this through again in terms of pers, beginning with the numerators. In a per representing something physical like wood or a wheel, the money numerators are always yes or no – one or zero, he thought. Money is just plain yes-or-no stuff. In fact, if a per with a money numerator happens to be in my who x when, it's because I already got to yes about it with someone else. So come to think of it, when I'm dealing with money, there's no zeros; money in my who x when is all yeses. Money represents a succession of transactional agreements.

Then Junior turned to the denominators of the pers, which represented things like wood and wheels. These were a little more complicated. First, on day one, he got to yes with someone else about how much wood there was – in stones. Then, on day three, when he sold a wheel, he got to yes with someone else – this time in wheels. And then there was the middle day.

If he were going to measure stuff on the middle day, he figured it would probably be at lunch when he wasn't working on the wheel, so he'd be about half done. He decided to write all this in a little model.

	Stones of Wood	Number of Wheels
Day 1	1	0
Day 2	1/2	1/2
Day 3	0	1

Junior's Table of Units of Denominator Measure

Hmm ..., Junior thought, transformation units of measure for denominator changes are in between zero and one because everything about a transformation can't be yes or no at the same time, and transformations occur a step at a time: a transformation is a sequenced process.

Junior concluded that Thogette had overdramatized the problem with his profit reports. During transformation, denominator in-betweens are linked by pers to money yeses throughout the process. It's only the denominators that are in between, not the whole per. The numerators are ones (yes = 1) every step of the way.

Junior decided to review his thinking with the family that evening.

"You see," he concluded his presentation, "units of denominator measure can be represented by numbers in between zero and one. But because of pers, these numbers are always linked to money numerators that are ones. Profit is not as bad a measure as Thogette made it sound."

"Oh my, yes!" Mrs. Thog exclaimed. "Your denominator measures between zero and one are measures of unconfirmed guesses! In-betweens are measures of uncertainty."

"Harumpf," said Thog, still partial to yes or nos.

"What should we call these measures, dear?" Mrs. Thog asked him.

"Well, it shouldn't be anything too fancy. The last thing we need to do here is overdignify guessing, even if it's just about denominators. How about calling them *in-betweens*?"

Mrs. Thog was more optimistic than Thog about measuring guesses. "After all, dear," she pointed out, "there is numerator uncertainty as well as denominator uncertainty.

Take the what x what. There are no guarantees about either the numerators or denominators of the pers in there. The what x what just reflects what things have fetched and might next fetch. And the numerators of many of the pers in the later-cells of the who x when are in-betweens as well, since they represent bites measuring incomplete transactions that may or may not be completed as agreed. For example, an account receivable for 100 beads might not be fully collected despite its having been transactionally confirmed at 100 beads. One might eventually collect only 80 beads or some lesser amount."

"I suppose," Thog grumbled. "At least all those amounts were previously yeses, or ones. Sometimes the numerators do get smaller as they shrink towards zero when things don't work out. But making them bigger than what has actually happened so far is sheer lunacy."

"Why yes, dear," Mrs. Thog said. "In-betweens are just a way to be a little more precise about your conservatism."

"I suppose. But one way or the other, when it comes to who x when recordkeeping, there will be an eventual day of yes-or-no reckoning for unresolved in-betweens."

At this point Bruce interjected. "I should think that adding unconfirmed yes-or-no numerator guesses in who x whens would create a combinatoric explosion of possibilities – maybe even a combinatoric disaster. If so, then Junior's observation that denominator in-betweens are contained by numerators that have already been transactionally confirmed would no longer be the case."

"Bright lad," Thog observed, approvingly.

Thogette smiled at Thog's approval.

"It's statistics!" Jim exclaimed. "The possible numbers in between zero and one are probabilities. For example, a yes-and-no possibility might have a 30% chance of being resolved yes and a 70% chance of being resolved no."

"Exactly," Mrs. Thog said.

"Aha!" Dr. Z exclaimed. "I'll bet probability was the epiphany."

"Almost, dear," Mrs. Thog said.

She resumed the story: It had taken Thogette a moment or two to compose a retort to Junior's presentation to the family, but eventually she came up with a pretty good one. "Well, Junior," she said, "if an in-between is so contained as you put it, then just how many possibilities would you suggest it has been limited to between zero and one?"

Junior paused. He almost fell for this, but he regained his balance and, grinning, replied: "Of course there are an infinite number of possibilities, but they are also contained between zero and one over time – you know, as in the concept of both – like yes and no – a paradox. Transformation measures are both infinite in possibility at any moment and sequentially contained by confirming transactions."

"Hmmpf!" Thogette replied.

"Hey, it was a clever shot, Thogette," said Bruce.

"Did I miss your epiphany, Mrs. Thog?" asked Dr. Z.

"Not really, dear. You see, for 50,000 years we used common sense to simplify a seemingly infinite complexity around us. Taking things a step at a time we got them down to yes or nos and kept track of these in our who x when. Then we realized that there is yet another infinity of possibilities between the steps, between the zeros and ones, within the who x when. Our epiphany was to realize that common sense is not only necessary when taking and measuring the steps, it's necessary when measuring between the steps while you are taking them. Our epiphany was nothing more earthshaking than to ratify the importance of common sense."

"As usual, she's right," Thog said. "You know," he continued, "speaking of metabolism and what you call 'haggle' ..."

"Were we speaking of metabolism and haggle, dear?" Mrs. Thog asked.

"Excuse me," he said, "I should have said speaking of common sense and in-betweens reminds me of metabolism and haggle. Agents in the haggler that are deciding whether to complete an exchange for something in their metabolic recipes must look in their what x whats to see what pers are involved. As you have pointed out, dear, the next per hasn't happened yet, so there is uncertainty. I was just thinking that it will take some arithmetic for an agent to aggregate what Jim calls the probabilities for each of the components in its metabolic recipe."

"Ah yes," Jim said. "We need to put the in-between arithmetic in the agent code."

"Absolutely," Bruce said.

"I'll do the code right now," Jim said.

"Can we put in common sense?" Dr. Z asked.

"No," Thog said. "But we can take a look and see which agents seem to be developing it."

Chapter 42

Zipfing Through Power Laws

Just when we wanted to try another particle collider run, a more pressing scientific problem arose and, in science, some things are even more important than experimentation, so we took first things first:

"You know," Bruce said, "I'm not sure the Lego™ possibilities loader is the very best name for the loader now."

"Perhaps not," Thog said, warming to a chance to rename it.

"The loader is beginning to look very biological," Stu said.

"Stu's right. Maybe we should call it the 'metabolic possibilities loader'," Thog said.

"Let's," said Bruce.

"What about the sign?" Sasha asked.

"The mathematical sign?" Jim said.

"No, the sign on the loader. It still says 'Lego™.'"

"Oh, I can take care of that," Thogette said, whipping out her drawing pencil and creating a new sign with artistic flair. "Your sign was ratty anyway, if you don't mind me saying so – I mean for such an important component of the particle collider."

With the loader renamed and the sign fixed, Thogette turned on the converter and, with our scientific priorities in order, we were now ready for some trial-and-error:

(all undergo standard collider drill)

Sasha: (watches agent monitor) Ura! Ura!

Junior: What?

Thogette: It means "hurray" in Russian.

Junior: Oh.

Sasha: (exclaims loudly) We have producers <u>and</u> consumers!

Stu: (watches macro monitor) And look – fitness landscapes. You can compare the financial positions of all the agents that are using the same currency.

Dr. Z: Yes, because you can review each agent's financial statements now that they're doing their own accounting.

Sasha: And look at this! The producers are distributed on a Zipf curve.

Dr. Z: Is that a good kind of curve to have in a particle collider?

Sasha: Oh, my yes. A Zipf curve shows how things like cities and firms are distributed in the real world – from large to small. It's a power law. George Zipf discovered in 1950 that word-usage frequency is distributed like this in languages. But any number of things are distributed like this. It's a very universal concept.

Dr. Z: (claps her hands) Oh, then it's working, it's working!

Bruce: (breaks out the champagne) It's time for a toast!

Jim: (turns on the toaster and turns off the collider) Absolutely!

(all indulge in various celebratory antics)

Stu: (professes) Ahem…this has some of the trappings of a primitive scientific success. But before we get too carried away with ourselves, let's review what we have and see what we're still missing.

(all return slowly to earth and begin cataloging the observed collider results)

Stu: (still professing) Let's see, we have agent producers and consumers, which appear to be interacting through haggle by exchanging particles and particle combinations. They appear to be learning from their experience and pursuing simple adaptive strategies. We have prices and exchange rates that appear to be resulting in the emergence of money, both as a measure and a medium of exchange. It appears that we're seeing currencies and currency communities emerge in power law configurations. We're also observing fitness landscapes for agents that share a common currency. So what are we missing?

Sasha: (disappointed) Of course, we haven't seen financial institutions – for example, a bank or stock market – complex firms, or any processes involving multiple metabolisms. And, of course, we haven't seen Schumpeterian gales. I'm afraid what we've modeled here is still a very primitive economy. We haven't saved economics as a science yet.

(everyone's mood chills)

Bruce: Hey, Sasha, don't take it so hard. It's been a long day. In fact, I'll tell you what. Why don't we all have dinner at my house? I'll cook.

Mrs. Thog: Why, what a lovely offer!

Thogette: (gazes at Bruce) Oh, and he cooks, too!

Stu: Oh yes, Bruce is a wonderful cook.

Thog: So Stu – how do you say it in biology – shall we go metabolize?

Stu: Let's!

Chapter 43

Concubines and Family Values

Bruce's Santa Fe house is small but it includes a state-of-the-art kitchen. Along with physics equations, quantum economics, and pipe organ concerts, Bruce loves recipes and cooking. And he was determined to reciprocate Thogette's haute couture of the evening before with his own haute cuisine.

The result was delightful: braised lamb shanks with spicily sautéed vegetables, a delicate salad, and a pear tart confection for dessert. He served us his last bottle of Chateau-Figeac premier grand cru classe de Saint-Emilion, his favorite wine. He wasn't surprised that Junior, in whose honor he'd served lamb, deferred in favor of Martinelli's nonalcoholic cider; after all he was there with his mom. But Thogette's deferral did surprise him after her performance the night before. It must be Thog's presence, he decided. Anyway Thog, Stu, and I made a fair-sized dent in the contents of Bruce's wine cellar that night, and Sasha helped, although he really prefers vodka.

After dinner the conversation returned to the particle collider and the statistical ramifications of in-betweens. But pretty soon we had changed topics again.

"Say," Bruce asked, "were you Thogs still in the Fertile Crescent when you figured out in-betweens?"

"Why yes," Mrs. Thog said, "but it was shortly after in-betweens that we decided to leave."

"Why was that?" Dr. Z asked.

"Perhaps we should skip that," Thog said, helping himself to a little more wine.

"Oh no, don't do that," Dr. Z said. "A step at a time – remember?"

So here's what they told us:

One night at dinner, and completely out of the blue, Thogette said, "Daddy, what's a concubine?"

Thog blushed and choked on a mouthful of food. Mrs. Thog and Junior immediately bent him over in a Thoglich maneuver.* After some dramatic thrashing about by Thog the food was dislodged and he could finally breathe as he tried to regain his sputtering composure.

There was silence at the Thogian table. Neither Mrs. Thog nor Junior looked as though they were going to help Thog out with Thogette's question, so he bit the bullet:

"Why, Thogette, whatever makes you ask?"

"I was looking at the elders' rules the other day and I noticed one of them that says men are entitled to have concubines."

"I see, and, may I ask, sweetie, why were you looking at the rules?"

"Oh, I was thinking about scaling up my banking activities. So I was checking the rules, and that's when I discov-

---

*Renamed the Heimlich maneuver and adopted by the American Red Cross in 1974.

ered this one. The rules present some obstacles to me scaling up banking, you know, at least here in our neighborhood."

"Ah yes," Thog said, hoping to change the subject. "Such as the rule against earning a profit from lending."

Mrs. Thog didn't care for the lending rules herself, but she frowned at Thog's attempt to divert Thogette from her question. The family has a tradition of intellectual honesty, the topic notwithstanding. Besides she'd already reviewed the birds-and-the-bees stuff with Thogette long ago.

Thog glanced at Junior again who was having trouble not smirking.

Thog slogged on. "You were wondering if the concubine rules might be an obstacle to banking?"

"Why yes, Daddy, I was," Thogette replied, "but it's hard to evaluate without knowing what a concubine is, of course."

"Let's see," Thog said, "perhaps the notion can be most clearly understood in terms of getting to yes or no about a per."

"Are you referring to a per as a relationship between two things, or between two people maybe?"

"Yes. For example, if one is the denominator in a yes or no pair and somehow ends up at yes and no about the numerator half of the pair, additional numerators that emerge are called 'concubines.'"

"Aren't you better off just getting to yes or no about your relationships a step at a time?" Thogette said.

"Why, yes, of course," Thog said. "Yes or nos reduce unnecessary complexity."

"Does it work the other way around? If I'm the numerator and I get to yes and no about my denominator, is a new denominator for me called a concubine?"

Mrs. Thog smiled and sat back in her chair. Junior giggled with delight.

"I don't believe those who wrote the rules on concubines expected their rule to work the other way around," Thog said, squirming in his chair.

"Is that what's known as a double standard?" Thogette asked. "Or perhaps the elders just haven't thought through their concubine rule thoroughly."

"I don't believe they have thought a number of their rules through thoroughly," Thog said.

"Yes," Thogette said, "I suppose if they had they wouldn't be putting so many guesses in who x whens now – what they're calling 'fair values.'"

Relieved at the change in subject, Thog said, "Yes, sweetie. In addition to the practices of keeping concubines and using fair values in who x whens, have you found other obstacles to scaling up your bank?"

Thogette smiled. She'd known all along what a concubine was. Bankers, after all, are worldly people. She just wanted to see how her father would handle the question. And, he hadn't done too badly, so she let him off the hook. "Yes, I have, Daddy. Would you like to discuss them?"

"Why, yes," Thog said, with a sigh of relief. "I'd like that very much!"

They then talked about various other obstacles to commercial scale in the Fertile Crescent such as the limitations on large commercial organizations, and the conversation might have gone on for a while, but Mrs. Thog cut it off by sending the children to bed a little early so she could discuss the implications of Thogette's question privately with Thog. And it was during this discussion that the Thogs decided to move from the Fertile Crescent to a better environment for raising their children – one that hopefully would be more accommodating of their commercial activities and the important roles in these activities played by Thogette and Mrs. Thog.

"The elders' rule that people had to use veils to cover any beads was a factor as well," Thog added, as the episode concluded. "Banking is veiled enough. Besides, Mrs. Thog is partial to beads and looks quite lovely wearing them."

Mrs. Thog blushed. "Well," she said, "we musn't overstay our welcome. Thank you so much for the lovely dinner, Bruce. Perhaps you'll share the recipe? The cuisine certainly exceeded the mere arithmetic sum of its parts."

"You're very welcome," Bruce said. "I'd be happy to share the recipe."

Chapter 44

Mrs. Thog's Book Club

The next morning we met for breakfast in a small cafe. Dr. Z, Mrs. Thog, and Thogette had granola. Stu, Thog, Junior, and I had bacon and eggs. Jim, Bruce, and Sasha had omelets – getting in the mood for metabolic equations, Bruce explained. And of course Jim ordered an extra side of toast.

As we were finishing our breakfast, I asked, "What about the rabbits?"

"Well," Mrs. Thog replied, "I guess this is as good a time as any to tell about the rabbits."

So we finally got to Fibonacci alias Leonardo's rabbits:

The Thogs had settled into their new home in the West and Mrs. Thog immediately made a number of friends. She's gregarious and likes to keep up with what's going on in the neighborhood. In talking with folks there, she learned about paper, invented in AD105. Immediately she saw paper's usefulness, it was lighter, easier to handle, and simpler to store than clay tablets, and it would make who x when recordkeeping a great deal easier. Mrs. Thog was disappointed that she hadn't learned about paper a thousand years earlier, when it was invented. For that matter, she wondered why the family hadn't thought of paper themselves. She resolved to redouble her efforts to keep up with the flow of interesting gossip around the neighborhood.

Which is how she happened to learn in 1202 of an interesting book by Leonardo Pisano called *Liber Abaci*.

"Do you know Leonardo Pisano, dear?" she asked Thog.

"Yes I do. Lovely fellow. We met in the recordkeeping underground. His name is actually Fibonacci, a contraction for son-of-Bonacio, I believe. Leonardo is just an alias. He's thoughtful, quite conversant with the who x when. No debits and credits for Fibonacci – he's an arithmetic man all the way."

"Speaking of arithmetic, I heard he made some very interesting computations involving a pair of breeding rabbits."

"Yes, I believe he computed the number of rabbits that will be born from a single pair over one hundred months, if rabbits breed every two months. The answer is a pretty big number, as I recall."

"I hope to shout," Jim interrupted. "Let me just compute it here on my palm pilot. I know the recipe – equation, if you prefer." He computed for a moment and announced: "The answer is 708,449,696,358,523,830,150 rabbits. You're right, Thog. It <u>is</u> a pretty big number."

"According to Fibonacci, we are going to have 708,449,696,358,523,830,150 babies around the house in a hundred months. So do you think we should get married?"

Continuing with the story, Mrs. Thog had said, "He's quite young, you know."

As usual, Mrs. Thog had her facts right: Fibonacci was in his early twenties when he did his rabbit work.

But Mrs. Thog had been unable to obtain a copy of Fibonacci's book. Since each book had to be handwritten, there were very few copies. And she thought it unfortunate that such a thoughtful young man had to spend time copying his work by hand, over and over. "He must get writer's cramp," she said. "It reminds me of who x when recordkeeping before Thogette invented numbers."

The family considered Fibonacci's problem. Thog thought a model for making books would be useful. Thogette thought such a model could be scaled-up, like a bank is scaled-up. Junior suggested some tools. And before you knew it, the Thogs had conceived printing to help circulate Leonardo's book.

But they didn't take up printing. Being conservative, Junior decided to stick with wheel-making. Thogette was pretty busy banking, although she did eventually bank a few printers. Thog preferred trading, or better yet, hunting. And Mrs. Thog was too busy with closing the who x when and periodic financial reporting to take on any extra printing chores.

But Mrs. Thog did love books, so she formed a neighborhood book club. In 1456, they read the *Gutenberg Bible*, the first best-seller in history. And in 1494, they read Luca Pacioli's *Summa*, a description of who x when recordkeeping that makes reference to Leonardo's earlier work on the same subject in *Liber Abaci*. Luca, however, was politically savvy and distanced himself from the who x when recordkeeping underground. He stuck with the politically fashionable terminology of the day, describing who x when recordkeeping instead as "double-entry accounting," and liberally sprinkling his *Summa* with debits and credits. The ladies enjoyed this book, although Mrs. Thog couldn't help chuckling a little over all the debits and credits.

Chapter 45

Commonsense Denominators

Mrs. Thog's book club had put us in a philosophical mood and we decided to walk to the secret laboratory while we digested our breakfast.

"I understand," Dr. Z said, "that some of your terminology stayed alive in the recordkeeping underground even though it was politically unpopular."

"Yes," Thog said. "It was particularly hard to keep a basic term like 'pers' underground."

Thogette picked up the story. "At the bank, when we reviewed a borrower's who x when to see if they were going to be able to pay back their loans, we used pers a lot. We expected accounts receivable to be per something exchanged with someone or some entity; inventories and property to be per something (a product, building, or some production activity); liabilities to be per something exchanged with someone; revenues to be per something sold; and expenses to be per something purchased (labor, services, products, or some productive activity). Successful banks routinely turned down borrowers who couldn't explain their pers, and banks that didn't often failed."

"Yes, money isn't everything," Mrs. Thog said. "And when it comes to financial statements it seems that people eventually come around to 'per what' questions about the money involved."

"Just asking 'per what?' isn't much use if the denominator answer to the question is garbled or ambiguous," Junior added. "It's important to be able to measure the answer. It's like a hunting story – I got 1 mastodon, 2 tigers, 20 rabbits."

"Yuk," Thogette said.

Junior ignored her. "Dad called denominators that you could measure *commonsense denominators*."

"Gosh," Dr. Z exclaimed, "it seems to me that commonsense denominators are out of fashion now. What's the denominator for the asset called 'capitalized research and development'? You can be required to show it in financial statements these days, but how does one count one unit of research and development? It's nothing more than a money measure waiting for a commonsense denominator."

"Well, Dr. Z," Thog said, "commonsense denominators do fall from fashion from time to time despite people asking 'money per what?' when confronted with financial statements expressed only in money."

"Denominators certainly remain popular in the scientific laboratory," Stu added.

"Yes," Jim said, "and speaking of the laboratory, here we are."

Chapter 46

Getting Past Primitive

We were all eager to run the particle collider. But, as Jim got organized Bruce asked the Thogs to tell us more about the Renaissance. "I used to be a professor, and the Renaissance was one of my favorite subjects to teach," he told Thogette.

"Oh my," Thogette said breathlessly, "a professor, too!"

The Thogs enjoyed the Renaissance. In 1543, Mrs. Thog's book club read *De Revolutionibus*, in which Copernicus suggested that the Earth and other planets revolve around the sun, instead of the other way around, and let me tell you, this resulted in a lively discussion down at the club that night.

In 1550, Junior enjoyed Cardano's *Liber de Ludo Aleae* on the statistical principles of probability, and reading it prompted him to refine his thinking about the statistical implications of his in-betweens.

Thog also read a few books, but he still preferred to read tracks and was beginning to complain; hunting during the Renaissance was not like the good old mastodon-hunting days.

Thogette's bank scaled better in the West than it had in the Fertile Crescent, but she had begun to worry about banking. In 1314, Philip IV of France executed the Templars, who were the bankers for the Crusades, and in 1343, Edward III of England defaulted on his loans, which resulted in the collapse of the Florentine banks: commonsense denominator problems. Banking started to look a little risky, so Thogette began to consider other lines of work, something appropriate for a young woman with 3,000 years of banking experience.

When she invented banking, Thogette used a model that simplified the who x when, focusing just on money. She wondered now if she could do something clever with the what x what, something that would scale-up like banking, but better preserve the advantage of her own who x when over others.

She considered what she'd learned from experience. When a borrower couldn't pay, the bank sometimes simply took their denominators, which were called "collateral." In some cases, in fact, the bank took all the denominators in a borrower's who x when. She figured that if ownership of an entire who x when could be transferred from one person to another, then it could also be divided into portions that could be bought and sold.

And of course any portion would be exactly the same as any other portion – one-tenth of something is exactly the samc as any other one tenth of it – so the portions would be exact common denominators.

"Aha!" she concluded. "Here's my idea: a what x what just for who x whens. That should make a very tidy little what x what. And Dad will love the common denominators."

As she considered this further, she realized that someone would have to keep track of who owned the various portions of any particular who x when, so her idea included devising a who x when for other who x whens as well. And besides it would be efficient if the people who were interested in exchanging who x when portions all came to the place where the what x what recordkeeping was done, thus simplifying route complexity and strengthening the position of whoever was doing the recordkeeping.

"Aha," I interrupted. "A natural monopoly."

"Yes," Thog said. "Thogette is commercially inclined, of course."

The story continued. Thogette realized that any who x when could be summarized by a financial statement and, now that printing had been invented, a number of people could read the financial statement for a who x when at the same time!

"This," she exclaimed, "is an even better idea than banking."

When Thogette explained her idea to the family, Junior said, "It's a good idea, but you sure get a lot of mileage out of using the same old 'just for this' and 'just for that' approach. First you came up with a who x when just for money, and now you've come up with a what x what just for who x whens."

"The application of simplifying correspondences to solve problems is called formulating a 'principle,'" Thogette huffed.

"Well, speaking of principles," Junior said, "I suppose you will then need a who x when for your what x what for just who x whens."

"Of course," Thogette replied. "Isn't it amazing how many commercial possibilities can be modeled with what x whats and who x whens?"

Thog thought Thogette's idea should be called a *stock market*,* because it's shorter than "Thogette's What x What for Just Who x Whens," not to mention catchier, and he thought the who x when portions should be called *shares*.

"Ura!" Sasha exclaimed. "There is hope! The particle collider will be able to construct financial institutions like stock markets from what x whats and who x whens."

"It's probably just as well you didn't name monopolies," I said to Thog. "They're not very popular these days."

"Yes," he said, "despite the fact that they often result in better products at lower prices."

"But when it comes to stock markets," Thogette said, "for some reason or other, even ardent anti-monopolists seem willing to look the other way."

"There is that," I admitted. "In my experience, they are different from software companies in that regard."

---

*Technically speaking, Thogette's what x what represented what today we call the "price discovery function" of a stock market, where bid and ask (quotes) and last trade are reported. Her who x when for shares in other who x whens performed account keeping and clearing functions that are no longer performed by modern stock markets, but by other institutions instead.

Chapter 47

Complex Metabolisms

Despite the possibility that the collider might produce financial institutions like stock markets, Sasha didn't stay optimistic for long. Before I'd even finished reminiscing on the topic of monopolies, he was worrying again.

"But, of course, just producing stock markets will be quite primitive," he said. "It still won't be much of an economy unless there are complex firms as well."

"Well, Sasha, I hate to be the one to bring this up," Thogette said, "but I think you should hear a little story about Junior before you give up hope completely."

So we postponed work on the particle collider once again to hear a little more about Junior:

With the Age of Discovery launched, thanks in no small part to Thogette's stock market, the Thogs enjoyed renewed prosperity. Meanwhile, Junior was thinking about his who x when. He needed something better than wheels to one-up Thogette's stock market, and in 1700 he decided to try something else.

He thought about how printers had achieved large-scale production by using tools and models. He wondered what else could be done with tools and models. He knew a little about wheels, and as the inventor of agriculture, he knew a little about crops, and as the inventor of in-betweens he knew a little about transformation processes. Let's see, he thought, there's corn, wheat, cotton, soybeans ... hmm ... maybe I could do something with cotton.

"I know what I can do!" he exclaimed. "I can link transformations! I can use a wheel to transform cotton to thread, and then transform thread to cloth, and cloth to clothing. And I can build a tool for each transformation step in the process."

Junior spent the remainder of the day fiddling around in his shop building some small-scale models of various possible tools, the best of which was a tool that automated the conversion of cotton to thread. He drew some sketches of this one.

Junior reviewed his idea with the family that night and explained how he planned to link transformation models in a single who x when. He showed them his sketch for a cotton transformation machine.

"It sounds like a magnificent idea to link transformation models," Mrs. Thog said.

"Yes," Thog said, "a capital idea!"

"Nice sketch," Thogette said, "although I could make a few suggestions about how you might improve it."

"Thanks anyway," Junior said. "The tool is the main thing, not the sketch of it."

"Well, how about some capital, then?" she said. "Would you like to float some shares on my stock market?"

"Now that," Junior replied, "I'd like."

Thog thought Junior's invention should be called an *assembly line*. It's shorter, and easier to say than "Junior's Who x When for Linked Transformation Processes."

"What a lovely name for a good idea," Mrs. Thog said, "I wouldn't be surprised to see any number of assembly lines before long."

"Were you right on, or what!" Bruce exclaimed. "By 1750, factories and the Industrial Revolution were in full swing."

"More important for us," Sasha added, "if the metabolisms in the collider are linked, it should produce assembly lines and complex firms."

"Speaking of the collider, isn't it time for another trial run?" Junior asked.

"Yes," Jim said, "but we've got some work to do first."

Chapter 48

Virtual Reality Accounting

Stu assumed the lead as we went to work on what the collider would need in order to produce stock markets and assembly lines.

"We need to link up some of these metabolisms," he said. "To begin with, an agent representing one metabolic possibility could learn of other metabolic possibilities through haggling with other agents."

"Yes, of course," Jim said. "That's exactly what happens in the real world. You learn new information by interacting with others."

"As its metabolic knowledge grows, an agent will need some way to keep track of it," Sasha said.

"Knowledge is a complex space down the line," Stu said, "extraordinarily complex."

"Yes," Mrs. Thog said, "but perhaps to begin with, the agents could just keep a little recipe book of their equations and take things a step at a time, metabolic equation by metabolic equation."

Everyone agreed with Mrs. Thog's suggestion, so Jim added a recipe book to the agent records.

"Do you think the haggler is really state of the art?" Thog asked.

"Not yet," Jim said.

"Perhaps you should consider adding some artificial intelligence," Thog suggested. "I'm sure Ray Kurzweil could help with that."

"Wow," Bruce said, "cool idea."

"Yes," Sasha said. "But since Ray's not here now, let's stick with successive Tit for Tat, and come back to that after we talk more with Ray."

"There's plenty of work to do right here." Jim said.

"For one thing," Bruce said, "our schematics are getting pretty messy – what with all the changes we've made – getting rid of the function generator and carbon absorber, adding what x whats and who x whens. Now that we're beginning to get to the bottom of this model and we're working on the agents and how they emerge, maybe you should just do an agent schematic."

"Good idea," Sasha said, and that's what he did.

Here's what it looked like:

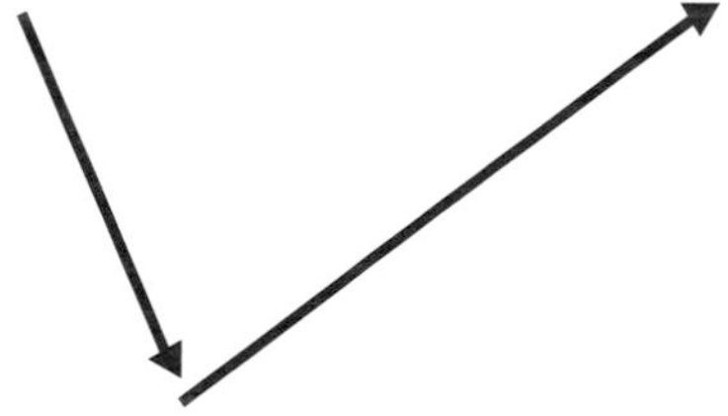

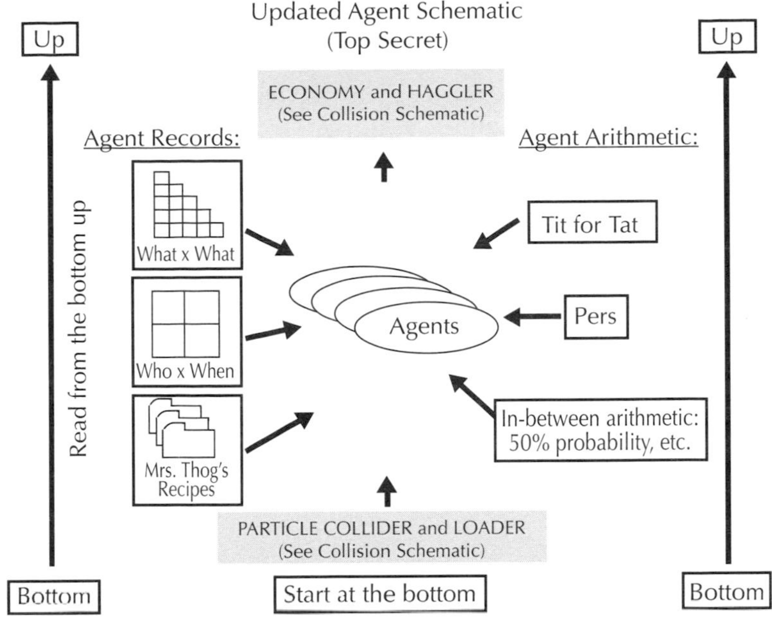

"We'll also need some way for an agent to buy another who x when," Dr. Z said. "According to the accounting rules, that requires purchase accounting. The purchaser records the acquiree at the price paid; if the purchaser pays in shares, that's the value of the shares it exchanges. The purchaser assigns any excess amount above the value of the net assets acquired to what is called 'goodwill.' For example, if one agent purchased another's assembly line containing 200 pounds of steel worth $100 dollars, and did so in exchange for shares in its own who x when worth $200, then it would record $100 worth of steel and $100 worth of goodwill. Once the collider has produced stock markets, the latest price of the shares exchanged will be available to both agents. What do you think?"

"Let's try it," Jim said, as he coded it up.

"Goodwill is a somewhat obscure denominator," Thog cautioned. But no one was listening. Everyone was anxious to run the collider again, and by now we were all watching Bruce set up the safety gear.

Thogette turned on the Kurzweil converter for the scientific record, and here's what happened next:

(all participate in standard collider drill)

Sasha: (watches the agent monitor) Look at these firms with multiple metabolisms.

Stu: (watches the macro monitor) Yes, and they're falling along power-law distributions, which continues to appear reassuring.

Brownie: (watches the agent monitor) Look! There's a bank and there's a stock market finally.

Thogette: Yes, that one still looks pretty primitive, but it is a stock market. Looks like they're still using specialists to me.

Brownie: (expresses relief) Then it's not NASDAQ.

(Collider runs faster)

Sasha: Maybe we're going to get a Schumpeterian gale now! I hope so!

(Collider begins to smoke)

Jim: I don't think so ...

Bruce: (shouts) Everybody get behind the Plexiglas shield!

(Collider whines loudly)

Bruce: (hits the emergency stop button) Emergency shutdown!

Thogette: (turns off the converter)

We had thought we were making great progress, so we were all terribly disappointed. The mood in the laboratory was somber.

"Perhaps you should rethink your accounting for the metabolic combinations," Mrs. Thog suggested.

"Yes," Thog said, "something more conservative, maybe."

"The only other way that I can think of to record combining who x whens is to simply add the purchaser's who x when to the acquiree's who x when and retain in each one the costs that have been transactionally verified in trade. This is called a pooling of interests, but poolings are no longer permitted by the latest accounting rules."

"Oh, they're still quite popular in the who x when recordkeeping underground," Mrs. Thog said. "Besides, I don't believe it's illegal to do them in a laboratory yet."

"Well, let's give that a try," Jim said. "It'll certainly be simpler to code."

So they did, and wouldn't you know it, the particle collider liked pooling better than purchase accounting? It hummed merrily along producing firms and financial institutions.

We spent a while enjoying our success, watching the monitors and talking about what we were seeing. But Sasha's attention had turned to the macro monitor. "Look at this," he suddenly shouted. "Messing around with all these accounting rules, I believe we're actually getting Schumpeterian gales over here!"

"Oh my," Dr. Z said, "the rules do seem to be affecting things economically. I guess they're not neutral like Switzerland after all."

"Huh?" Bruce asked. "What's Switzerland have to do with this?"

"Oh, it's just something the accounting regulators like to say about their rules," said Dr. Z.

Sasha began dancing around the macro monitor. Up till now, Dr. Z held the record in our group for extreme emotive response to scientific results, but the gales sent Sasha right past her like a rocket headed for space with a satellite to deliver. His enthusiasm was infectious, and pretty soon Dr. Z was whooping away, too.

Eventually Sasha and Dr. Z came back down to earth, and Dr. Z asked if it would be possible to try out another accounting policy, now that we had tested purchase versus pooling accounting.

"Virtual reality accounting," Thog said. "We're trying out accounting rules in virtual reality – just like how Ray and I went mastodon hunting."

"Why, yes," Mrs. Thog said.

"Could we test stock option accounting?" Dr. Z asked. "There's such a hullabaloo about it."

"So I've read," Mrs. Thog said. "I understand that employees are often given options to purchase shares in the company where they work. They have the right to purchase the shares later but at the price the shares fetched when the option was granted. Is that right?" she asked.

"Yes," Dr. Z said.

"I understand the accounting rule for recording these options requires the company to guess, at the time the option is granted, what the option will be worth later, when and if the employee exercises it, and then record this guess as compensation expense in their financial statements. Am I correct?" Mrs. Thog asked.

"Yes, quite," Dr. Z affirmed. "Except there are also rules about exactly how much the guess must be."

"Say what?" Jim said. "How am I ever gonna code that?"

"Oh, the rules specify the formulas to be used," she said. "I have one of them right here in my backpack – it's called the Black-Scholes equation."*

"Aren't those the guys who got the Nobel Prize for their guessing formula and then made such a big mess on Wall Street when they tried to use it themselves?" Thogette asked.

"Well, there is that," Dr. Z said.

"This thing is gonna take some coding," Jim said as he looked over the complex formula. "You're gonna have to give me some time here."

---

*The Black-Scholes equation:

$$C = S \times N(D) - Ke^{-rt} \times N(D - \sigma \sqrt{t}), \text{ where } D = \frac{\ln\left(\frac{S}{K}\right) + \left(r + \frac{\sigma^2}{2}\right) t}{\sigma \sqrt{t}}$$

Note: For those who like to know all the details of a complex guess: C is the call option; S is the market price of the underlying stock; N(z) is the cumulative normal distribution function evaluated at "z"; K is the exercise price; e is the base of the natural logarithm, a constant with a value of approximately 2.718282; r is the continuous compounding riskless interest rate; t is the time to option expiration (√ indicates the square root of t); σ is the annualized standard deviation of the rate of return on the stock, referred to as the asset price volatility; and ln(z) indicates the natural logarithm function evaluated at "z." Of course, even if you know the big words for all the symbols, your guess can still be wrong.

So we sat around the collider drinking coffee and watching Jim code up Black-Scholes. This led to a discussion of long formulas. Stu, Bruce, and Sasha knew a couple of doozies, which they entertained us with while we waited for Jim to finish.

When Jim was ready to go, we fired up the collider. But this time Thogette hadn't even turned on the Kurzweil converter before the collider began to slow down. It ran slower and slower and within a minute or two it had locked up entirely.

"It's way deep in the ordered regime," Bruce said.

"I don't get it," Dr. Z said. "We put purchase accounting rules in here and this thing goes combinatoric. Then we put stock option accounting rules in and it plunges deep in the ordered regime. What's going on here?"

"When the rules require fair value accounting the operating results can become random, with multidirectional consequences," Mrs. Thog observed philosophically.

"Worse, they're usually followed by rabbit hunting," groused Thog.

At this point it looked as if we'd finally followed the combinatoric tracks all the way back around to the rabbits, so we decided to call it a day on trial-and-error with the particle collider.

Chapter 49

Rabbits and Schumpeterian Gales

"Ah yes, rabbits." Stu said. "Perhaps we should hear about them over dinner and digest what we've been learning in the laboratory for the last several days."

"A capital idea!" Thog said.

"I know a great French restaurant," Bruce said.

"Oh, Bruce," Thogette interrupted, casting a cautious glance in her father's direction, "perhaps we should try somewhere new tonight."

"Of course," he replied quickly. (Quantum physicists are sensitive to subtlety.) "I know a great Mexican place."

Soon we found ourselves munching nachos and salsa, listening to the final episode in the Thogs' story. And if you hadn't had dinner with her the night before last, you might have thought Thogette was just another teenager out with her parents for Mexican food.

"What is this thing about rabbit hunting?" I asked.

The Thogs explained that the Schumpeterian gale of 1929 was quite a storm. Disturbed by various bad accounting practices involving guesses, however, they had anticipated the storm, cleaned up all their commercial undertakings, and returned to hunting and gathering. As a result, when the storm hit they were able to wait it out safely, but there wasn't much left to hunt except rabbits. When they sensed the beginning of another bad-accounting-rabbit-hunting cycle coming on in 1999, the family moved near Santa Fe. Thog went on to explain that this bad-accounting-rabbit-hunting cycle had occurred a number of times, and over the years he had developed an aversion to rabbit hunting.

"1929 wasn't the first gale we experienced," added Mrs. Thog, who took a few moments to fill in the historical record of recessions and recoveries between their time in the Fertile Crescent and the Great Depression.

"Maybe we can start to understand these gales better now," Sasha said, "now that we can begin to model them."

"They seem to follow an explosion of in-betweens," Thog observed. "When you get a lot of new transformations linked up, things grow complex and there are a lot of in-betweens. Nowadays things are even more complex than they were during the Industrial Revolution. Now transformations are linked in a web, rather than in a straight line like the first assembly lines. Anyway, after a big change like the assembly line or the World-Wide Web, sometimes there's just a lot of unresolved ambiguity – transactionally speaking, of course – and this unsettles the economic weather."

"Yes," Mrs. Thog added, "and when denominator transformations become more uncertain, for some reason or other the accounting standard-setters seem to make matters worse by requiring more and more numerator guesses in who x whens, which just complicates the problem."

"Yes," Thog said, "and in our experience, when they begin doing that it's about time to get back to hunting and gathering."

"And how about the end of your virtual reality mastodon hunt with Ray?" I asked Thog.

"Ah yes," he said leaning back and taking up the story ...

But I'm going to spare you the final details of their hunt, since you'll have to admit, a mastodon hunt is a little far afield in a serious book about complexity science accounting and quantum economics. Besides, this story has gone on long enough, and if you want to know what a mastodon hunt is really like, you should experience one for yourself. Maybe Mrs. Thog could finagle a hunt with Ray for you.

Chapter 50

Back on Wall Street

After we finished our interviews with the Thogs, Dr. Z flew to California and returned to her university. Before she left she showed me the last entry in her diary. It read:

Dear Diary,

I'm learning to live in a paradoxical world. And the ultimate paradox is that I never should have changed my major. I should have majored in science to understand accounting!

So I wasn't surprised to hear that Dr. Z has been hanging around the physics department and evangelizing the use of consequential simulation models to test accounting rules – virtual reality accounting, she calls it. Her cause hasn't proved very popular with the accounting standard-setters, who, much as Chief Left-It did, continue to dismiss uncertainty and seem to still have the intelligence problem that Ray Kurzweil mentioned to Thog after the virtual reality mastodon hunt – knowing what not to compute. But you know Dr. Z; when she sets her mind to something she can be pretty determined. So it's premature to bet against her.

As for me, I flew home to New York and went back to work at NASDAQ. When various colleagues asked me how my vacation had been, I decided it would be wisest simply to summarize: very interesting, spent a little time with some scientists, got some fresh air, heard some new ideas that really weren't that new – that sort of thing.

But I had trouble getting back into the rhythm of my work. I'd come to think of it as what x what for who x whens work, and I began having unsettling dreams at night about models, guesses, gales, rabbits, and whatnot.

One day a few weeks later, I was sitting in my office when my administrative assistant poked her head in the door and announced: "There's a Professor Anderson on the line for you."

"Who?" I asked through the door.

"Says he's a PartEcon fisheries biologist. Says he's collaborating with some scientists on an interdisciplinary project involving salmon. Says he wants to talk about measuring how salmon haggle – some mumbo jumbo about whats and whos and whens, more work to do on haggle, that sort of thing. I told him you were busy. Shall I biff him, so you can get some work done?"

"Ahh, fish? No … don't biff him. In fact, maybe you'd better put him on."

"Oh, and by the way, there's a young lady on the other line who says her name's Thogette. Now she sounds like she knows a thing or two about markets, this one does. She says she wants to talk about the climate on the street, something about the weather getting worse."

"On second thought, keep Professor Anderson on the line and let me see what Thogette has to say. But don't let Professor Anderson get away."

"Play him like a fish, huh?" (giggle).

"Yeah, like a fish."

Soon after, I got out of the stock market business. Thogette's warning call was prescient. A few months after I left, the weather on Wall Street began to change. At first it was just a gray drizzle, but before long it had built into the biggest gale since 1929. I'm not much of a rabbit hunter, so I decided to go fishing, though my fishing skills were a bit rusty.

I turned to Thog for advice.

"I was worried about all the guesses – you know, fair value accounting, its effects on the stock market, that sort of thing," I explained to him. "I decided to go fishing and wait it out. The problem is, I'm not catching much fish."

"I'm sorry, but I can't help you. I'm a hunter myself," Thog said. "Perhaps you should consult with Professor Anderson – he's working on how fish haggle, you know. Of course, you could also practice in virtual reality. Ray would be helpful for that."

As to guesses, fair values, and accounting, Thog went on to reassure me – just as he had reassured Mrs. Thog, Thogette, and Junior on the trail to Santa Fe – the basic models are still sound. "Most people grow out of fair value accounting eventually," he said. "Like Junior and Dr. Z outgrew debits and credits. Common sense will come back in fashion and people will get back to accounting with real bites – bites that have been confirmed in an actual transaction. Maybe not overnight. When there is a gale, you just have to be a little patient."

Armed with Thog's reassurances, a little advice from Professor Anderson, some virtual reality practice with Ray, and patience, I've continued to reflect on the nature of haggle and my catch has been slowly improving.

"The fishing report did mention something about Schumpeterian conditions."

Afterword

I'm Warren Miller, back for another word. I thought you might enjoy knowing what some of the characters in the story are doing now:

PartEcon is alive, but just barely. The Particle Economics Research Institute is a non-profit skunk works dedicated to improving the economic particle collider. This of course eventually takes money from somewhere else since there aren't any profits, and PartEcon is looking for money. A portion of the proceeds from the sale of this book will be used to continue its work on the collider, or if there isn't enough for that, at least to buy a broom. The laboratory is more ramshackle than ever, and both Mrs. Thog and Dr. Z have this thing about tidiness.

In *Thog's Guide*, the collider's capabilities were exaggerated in the name of fiction, always popular in accounting. In truth, there is more work to do on haggle, and virtual reality accounting as described in Chapter 48 remains on the horizon of scientific possibilities. With that said, there really is a Collider, and it has produced emergent money and power law patterns – primitive results.

Mike Brown (Brownie) is retired and currently sailing the ocean, where he says he is studying haggle and fishing, with his wife, Lee. He serves on several boards as well as on the science staff at PartEcon.

Zoe-Vonna Palmrose (Dr. Z) lives with her husband, John, in the San Juan Islands in Washington State. She still teaches accounting at USC, but is spending more time in quantum economics, and is the president of PartEcon.

Stuart Kauffman lives with his wife, Liz, in Santa Fe. The author of numerous papers and books, Stu continues his groundbreaking work on the origins of biological life. He is the chairman of PartEcon. Oh, and he really can yodel!

Jim Herriot lives with his wife, Maren, in Palo Alto. He does private consulting in complexity science and is chief computer guru at PartEcon.

Bruce Sawhill lives in California and has been spending a lot of time with Thogette these days. When he can find time, he works with Jim doing private consulting in complexity science and is chief physicist at PartEcon.

Sasha Outkin lives with his wife, Vlada, and their baby daughter, in Los Alamos, New Mexico, where he works at the Los Alamos National Lab and is chief economist at PartEcon.

Ray Kurzweil lives with his wife, Sonya, in Boston. One of the world's leading technology futurists, Ray is an advisor to PartEcon. He invented the Kurzweil keyboard and Kurzweil reading machine for the visually impaired, and has started nine technology companies by last count, all successful. Ray has written numerous papers and books. In addition to receiving the National Medal of Technology in 1999, he has been awarded the Lemuelson-MIT Prize for technology and innovation in 2001, and was inducted into the Inventors Hall of Fame in 2002. Oh, and his alter-ego really is Ramona, in case you didn't have a chance to meet her at www.KurzweilAI.net. She not only sings and dances, she composes as well.

Jim Anderson lives in Seattle with his wife, Michele, where he directs Columbia Basin Research at the University of Washington's School of Aquatic and Fishery Sciences and works on agent-based modeling of fish behaviors specializing in the mathematics of fish haggle. He is on the science staff of PartEcon where he is working on a secret new particle spawner.

Thog, Mrs. Thog, Thogette, and Junior continue to live in the mountains outside of Santa Fe keeping an eye on accounting developments. They are all members of the PartEcon science staff now. Mrs. Thog stays busy with her who x when recordkeeping. Thogette and Junior are getting along better than usual, perhaps because Thogette is gone a lot – off with Bruce – although she still competes with Junior as to who will invent what next. Thog has been spending more time with Ray Kurzweil – planning a saber tooth tiger hunt now – or at least so I heard.

As for my wife, Laurie, and myself, we summer in the San Juans and ski Yellowstone Mountain in the winter. In fact, if you ever get to Yellowstone and happen to see a bunch of folks in white lab coats out carving up the powder, it's probably just me (yes, I have my own lab coat now) and the PartEcon gang taking a break from quantum economics. (The one doing back-flips off the moguls is usually Junior.)

Who would have thought common sense was the key to something like quantum economics? Not me, I can tell you. But thanks to the Thogs, now even an old ski bum like me can lend a hand in science once and a while.

Oh, and if <u>you</u> would like to interview the Thogs, just take a walk in the mountains outside Santa Fe and listen carefully. You might hear Thog and Stu yodeling to one another, and then you can track them down for yourself.

Thogesaurus

Account – a subset of any of the four basic addresses in a who x when (e.g. account receivable, cash, equity, inventory, etc.).

Address – a specific location on a map or in a model.

Agent – in agent-based modeling, a proxy for an individual which can act on its own behalf.

Agent-based models – computational simulations of the global consequences of interactions between individual agents.

Agriculture – a model for producing crops and tending livestock.

Arithmetic (mathematics) – computing with numbers that can be represented by symbols.

Assembly line – a model of linked transformations.

Banking – the creation of money using plusses and minuses in a who x when.

Before now – two of the four primary addresses of the who x when, comprising an income statement.

Bit – a yes or no, the smallest unit of information in information theory.

Bite – a yes or no, the smallest practical component of a transaction represented by a number pair.

Bulla – a clay ball for a bite filled with tokens representing its number pair.

Byte – a cluster of eight bits, a popular portion size with computers.

Closing the who x when – cleaning up your cave periodically by getting rid of outdated denominators.

Combinatorics – the branch of mathematics dealing with combinations of objects in accordance with specified constraints.

Commonsense denominators – yes or no answers to per what questions that arise in the interpretation of financial statements, except in fair value regulatory accounting where common sense is discouraged.

Conservatism – not measuring profits in your who x when until you're pretty sure they already happened.

Credit – softer-sounding word for minus, suitable for explaining who x when recordkeeping to children before they become comfortable with arithmetic.

Debit – softer-sounding word for plus, suitable for explaining who x when recordkeeping to children before they become comfortable with arithmetic.

Decoherence – getting from yes <u>and</u> no to yes <u>or</u> no.

Denominator – the bottom half of a per that names or nominates what has been measured.

Fair values – 1. Chief Left-It's words for a guess as to what something might fetch in a subsequent transaction. 2. Fair market value accounting – accounting with guesses.

Fence – an address identifier in an agriculture model.

Fitness – a central concept in evolutionary biology measuring the capability of an individual of a certain genotype to reproduce.

Fitness landscape – a measure of the extent to which a genotype is flourishing.

Garden – Mrs. Thog's model for growing plants.

Getting to yes or no – (from yes and no) – quantum decoherence or disambiguation.

Guess – a prediction as to how much money a denominator will fetch in the future; in regulatory accounting, also known as a fair value.

Half is as good as it gets – the application of the Heisenberg Uncertainty Principle to financial statements, due to the use of arithmetic.

In-betweens – a measure of probability between one and zero, as in $\frac{1}{2}$ or 50%, etc.

Later – a time in the future when a transaction will be consummated.

Map – a model of where things are located.

Mine later – a principle address in the who x when, also known as assets.

Mine now – a principle address in the who x when, also known as revenues.

Minus – the name for the symbol "-" that represents subtraction.

Model – a symbolic representation.

Money – a standard that serves as both a measure and a medium of exchange.

Nominal – in who x when recordkeeping, a small numerator that is not easily confused with a guess.

Now – the moment at which a transaction is agreed upon.

Numerator – the top half of a per that numbers or measures something.

Per – 1. a fraction, or ratio. 2. *Per what*? A question as to the denominators represented by money when money serves as a measure; useful in financial statement interpretation, except in regulatory accounting where you usually can't tell.

Plus – the name for the symbol "+" that represents addition.

Power law – in mathematics, a relationship between two quantities such that one is proportional to a fixed power of the other.

Profit (or *loss*) – the arithmetic sum of the before now addresses in a who x when.

Proper – an adjective favored by moms and regulatory accountants, used to describe what pleases them.

Recipe – an equation.

Route complexity – also known as The Traveling Salesman problem; occurs because there are a large number of possible routes between even a relatively small number of possible destinations.

Schumpeterian gales – in economics, the notion articulated by Joseph Schumpeter that "gales of creative destruction" occur in which obsolete firms fail and are succeeded by those with new technologies.

Shares – portions of a who x when.

Standard – a yes or no record of a past notion for future use.

Stick – see tally stick.

Stick complexity – complexity from too many sticks.

Stock market – a what x what for who x when shares.

Take or trade problem – (also known as The Prisoner's Paradox or The Prisoner's Dilemma). A negative stalemate.

Tally stick – a piece of wood or bone with carved notches that represent a number. Useful in starting a transaction now that will not be completed until later.

Token – a clay object, or standard, representing an idea.

Transformation – a change in a physical object occasioning a change in units of its measure.

Trial and error method – the scientific method.

Up to now – two of the four primary addresses in the who x when, representing bites in transactions consummated up to now.

What x what – a model of possible relationships between pairs.

Who x when – the conceptual framework for financial statements, except in regulatory accounting where the regulators have their own.

Win-win – in game theory (also known as Tit for Tat), a strategy for cooperative, interactive behavior.

Writing – using symbols to represent ideas.

Yes and no – something in an ambiguous state.

Yes or no – a binary question.

Yours later – a principle address in the who x when, also known as liabilities.

Yours now – a principle address in the who x when, also known as expenses.

Zero – the name for the symbol "0", representing nothing where something might have been before.

The Contents of Dr. Z's Backpack

Dr. Z organizes her backpack by topic. An alphabetic listing follows her summary.

Accounting: Canning (1929), Chatfield (1977), Cripps (1994), Ellerman (2004), Hendricksen (1965), Jacobsen (1964), Jones (1956), Keister (1963), Laing (2000), Littleton and Yamey (1956), May (1936), Previts and Merino (1998), Robert (1956), Zeff (1972)

Art and Civilization: Beckett (1994), Boorstin (1983), Roberts (1998), Van Doren (1991)

Classics: Cardano (1663), Copernicus (1543), Fibonacci (1202), Gutenberg (1456), Pacioli (1494)

Complexity Science: Casti (1994), Epstein (1996), Ernst & Young (1996), Holland (1995, 1998), Johnson (2001), Kauffman (1993, 1995, 2000), Pagels (1998), Waldrop (1992)

Fiction: Brinley (1961, 1968), Carrol (1872), Stephenson (1999), Weisbecker (2001)

Finance and Economics: Bernstein (1996), Cohen (1992), Galbraith (1975), Kindleberger (1993), Kuran (2001), Schumpeter (1942), Weatherford (1997), Wriston (1992)

Quantum Physics: Greene (1999), Smolin (1997, 2001), Zukav (1980)

Science, Math, and Technology: Clawson (1994), Cole (1998), Kurzweil (1990, 1999), Morange (1998), Peat (2002), Poundstone (1992), Seife (2000), Struik (1987), Watson (1980)

Beckett, Sister Wendy. *The Story of Painting: The Essential Guide to the History of Western Art*. (London: Dorling Kindersley, 1994).

Bernstein, Peter L. *Against the Gods: The Remarkable Story of Risk*. (New York: John Wiley & Sons, Inc., 1996).

Boorstin, Daniel J. *The Discoverers: A History of Man's Search to Know His World and Himself*. (New York: Random House, 1983).

Brinley, Bertrand R. *The Mad Scientists' Club*. (Keller, Texas: Purple House Press, 1961).

Brinley, Bertrand R. *The New Adventures of the Mad Scientists' Club*. (Keller, Texas: Purple House Press, 1968).

Canning, John B. *The Economics of Accountancy: A Critical Analysis of Accounting Theory*. (New York: The Ronald Press Company, 1929).

Cardano, Girolamo. *Liber de Ludo Aleae.* (written in 1525 but not published until 1663).

Carrol, Lewis. *Through the Looking Glass (And What Alice Found There).* (1872).

Casti, John L. *Complexification: Explaining a Paradoxical World Through the Science of Surprise.* (New York: HarperPerennial, 1994).

Chatfield, Michael. *A History of Accounting Thought (Revised Edition).* (Huntington, New York: Robert E. Krieger Publishing Company, 1977).

Clawson, Calvin C. *The Mathematical Traveler: Exploring the Grand History of Numbers.* (New York: Plenum Press, 1994).

Cohen, Edward E. *Athenian Economy & Society: A Banking Perspective.* (Princeton, New Jersey: Princeton University Press, 1992).

Cole. K. C. *The Universe and the Teacup: The Mathematics of Truth and Beauty.* (New York: Harcourt Brace & Company, 1998).

Copernicus, Nicolaus. *De Revolutionibus.* (1543).

Cripps, Jeremy. *Particularis de Computis et Scripturis, A Contemporary Interpretation.* (Seattle: Pacioli Society, 1994).

Ellerman, David. "Generalized Double-Entry Accounting: Showing What is 'Double' in the Double-Entry Method." University of California at Riverside Department of Economics working paper (2004).

Epstein, Joshua M. and Robert Axtell. *Growing Artificial Societies: Social Science from the Bottom Up*. (Washington, D.C.: The Brookings Institution Press, 1996).

Ernst & Young. *Embracing Complexity: Exploring the Application of Complex Adaptive Systems to Business* (A Summary of the 1996 Colloquium on the Business Application of Complexity Science). (The Ernst & Young Center for Business Innovation).

Fibonacci or Leonardo of Pisa. *Liber Abaci*. (1202).

Galbraith, John Kenneth. *Money: Whence It Came, Where It Went*. (Boston: Houghton Mifflin Company, 1975).

Greene, Brian. *The Elegant Universe*. (New York: W. W. Norton & Company, 1999).

Gutenberg, Johann. The Gutenberg *Bible,* printed before 1456.

Hendricksen, Eldon S. *Accounting Theory*. (Homewood, Illinois: Richard D. Irwin, Inc., 1965).

Holland, John H. *Emergence: From Chaos to Order.* (Reading, Massachusetts: Perseus Books, 1998).

Holland, John H. *Hidden Order: How Adaptation Builds Complexity.* (Reading, Massachusetts: Perseus Books, 1995).

Jacobsen, Lyle E. "The Ancient Inca Empire of Peru and the Double Entry Accounting Concept." *Journal of Accounting Research*. (Autumn 1964): 221-228.

Johnson, Steven. *Emergence: The Connected Lives of Ants, Brains, Cites, and Software*. (New York: Touchstone, 2001).

Jones, Tom. "Bookkeeping in Ancient Sumer." *Archaeology.* (March 1956): 16-21.

Kauffman, Stuart. *At Home in the Universe*. (New York: Oxford University Press, Inc., 1995).

Kauffman, Stuart. *Investigations*. (New York: Oxford University Press, Inc., 2000).

Kauffman, Stuart. *Origins of Order*. (New York: Oxford University Press, Inc., 1993).

Keister, O. R. "Commercial Record-Keeping in Ancient Mesopotamia." *The Accounting Review.* (April 1963): 371-377.

Kindleberger, Charles P. *A Financial History of Western Europe (Second Edition)*. (New York: Oxford Press, 1993).

Kuran, Timur. "The Islamic Commercial Crisis: Institutional Roots of the Delays in the Middle East's Economic Modernization." USC Center for Law, Economics & Organization Research Paper No. C01-12 (March 2001).

Kurzweil, Ray. *The Age of Intelligent Machines.* (Boston: The MIT Press, 1990).

Kurzweil, Ray. *The Age of Spiritual Machines.* (New York: The Penguin Group, 1999).

Laing, Jonathan R. "The New Math: Why an Accounting Guru Wants to Shake Up Some Basic Tenets of His Profession." *Barron's.* (November 20, 2000): 31-36.

Littleton, A. C. and B. S. Yamey. *Studies in the History of Accounting.* (Homewood, Illinois, Richard D. Irwin, Inc., 1956).

May, George O. *Twenty-Five Years of Accounting Responsibility: 1911-1936.* Edited by Bishop Carleton Hunt. (New York: Price Waterhouse & Co., 1936).

Morange, Michel. *A History of Molecular Biology.* (Cambridge, MA.: Harvard University Press, 1998).

Pacioli, *Luca. Summa de Arithmetica, Geometria, Proportioni et Proportionalita.* (1494).

Pagels, Heinz. *The Dreams of Reason.* (New York: Simon and Schuster, 1998).

Peat, F. David. *From Certainty to Uncertainty: The Story of Science and Ideas in the Twentieth Century.* (Washington, D.C.: Joseph Henry Press, 2002).

Poundstone, William. *Prisoner's Dilemma*. (New York: Doubleday, 1992).

Previts, Gary John and Barbara Dubis Merino. *A History of Accountancy in the United States: The Cultural Significance of Accounting*. (Columbus, Ohio: Ohio State University Press, 1998).

Robert, Rudolph. "A Short History of Tallies." in *Studies in the History of Accounting*. Edited by A. C. Littleton and B. S. Yamey. (Homewood, Illinois: Richard D. Irwin, Inc., 1956): 76-85.

Roberts, J. M. *A Short History of the World*. (New York: Oxford University Press, 1998).

Schumpeter, Joseph A. *Capitalism, Socialism and Democracy.* (New York: Harper Colophon Books, 1942).

Seife, Charles. *Zero: The Biography of a Dangerous Idea.* (New York: Penguin Books, 2000).

Smolin, Lee. *The Life of the Cosmos*. (New York: Oxford University Press, 1997).

Smolin, Lee. *Three Roads to Quantum Gravity.* (New York: Basic Books, 2001).

Stephenson, Neal. *Cryptonomicon*. (New York: Perennial, 1999).

Struik, Dirk J. *A Concise History of Mathematics (Fourth Revised Edition)*. (New York: Dover Publications, Inc., 1987).

Van Doren, Charles. *A History of Knowledge*. (New York: Ballantine Books, 1991).

Waldrop, M. Mitchell. *Complexity: The Emerging Science at the Edge of Order and Chaos*. (New York: Simon & Schuster, 1992).

Watson, James D. *The Double Helix: A Personal Account of the Discovery of the Structure of DNA*. Text, Commentary, Reviews, and Original Papers edited by Gunther S. Stent. (New York: W. W. Norton & Company, 1980).

Weatherford, Jack. *The History of Money*. (New York: Three Rivers Press, 1997).

Weisbecker, A. C. *Cosmic Banditos*. (New York: New American Library, 2001).

Wriston, Walter B. *The Twilight of Sovereignty: How the Information Revolution is Transforming Our World*. (New York: Charles Scribner's Sons, 1992).

Zeff, Stephen A. *Forging Accounting Principles in Five Countries: A History and an Analysis of Trends*. (Champaign, Illinois: Stipes Publishing Company, 1972).

Zukav, Gary. *The Dancing Wu Li Masters: An Overview of the New Physics*. (New York: Bantam Books, 1980).